`QUEEN ELIZABETH´
at war

'QUEEN ELIZABETH'
at war
HIS MAJESTY'S TRANSPORT 1939~1946

CHRIS KONINGS
with sketches by Oswald Brett

foreword by Frank O. Braynard

afterword by Walter Lord

PSL Patrick Stephens, Wellingborough

To the memory of my father
Arend Konings
from whom I inherited a
life-long love for ships.

First published 1985

British Library Cataloguing in Publication Data

Konings, Chris
'Queen Elizabeth' at War
1. Queen Elizabeth *(Ship)*
2. World War, 1939-1945—Naval Operations,
British   3. World War, 1939-1945—Personal
narratives
I. Title
940.54'5941'0922   D722.Q4

ISBN 0-85059-725-0

Patrick Stephens Limited is part of the
Thorsons Publishing Group.

Text photoset in 11 pt Plantin
by Manuset Limited, Baldock, Herts.
Printed in Great Britain on 135 gsm Fineblade coated
cartridge, and bound, by Butler & Tanner Limited,
Frome, Somerset, for the publishers,
Patrick Stephens Limited, Denington Estate,
Wellingborough, Northants,
NN8 2QD.

Contents

Foreword by Frank O. Braynard

Great ships do not die. They live on and on, in memories of people who knew them, in paintings and sketches by artists who drew them and in fine books such as this. On all three counts, in fact, this work will do much to further enshrine the saga of the great Cunard Line trans-Atlantic liner *Queen Elizabeth*. Chris Konings is to be congratulated for all the effort he put into his work about war service of this great ocean liner.

The *Queen Elizabeth* will probably be remembered by many as the largest passenger ship ever built. Although she was only a few gross tons larger than the famous French *Normandie*, her title as 'the largest of all time' will ensure her immortality. Her post-war service was important in the story of the 'Ocean Ferry'. She came to be loved by many thousands of happy voyagers.

But it was her war service which will be best remembered and which is featured in this work. Built on the eve of World War 2, no one knew what would be her fate. It became obvious that she could not be used in peaceful trades and she was rushed to completion in great secrecy. I was at my home on Long Island the day she suddenly arrived at the Narrows on the completion of her first trans-Atlantic crossing. No one had expected her. Her passage was a well-kept British Navy secret. Her crew had been signed on for a short delivery trip from Scotland to England. They were only told that their destination was New York after the ship had set sail. My radio told me the news of her arrival. I dropped everything and rushed to the railroad station heading for New York. What a sight she was! I first glimpsed her from the deck of a Staten Island ferry. I rode it back and forth until I had my fill of her massive grey bulk.

The war story of the *Queen Elizabeth* is well worth telling. No one can say how the war itself might have turned out had the Allies not had this great ship and her companion vessel—the famed *Queen Mary*. She was able to carry a full division, 16,000 men, in one voyage. Her great speed helped earn for her one of the most heroic and successful careers as a troop carrier in World War 2. She was seen on every ocean around the world. This book can only begin to touch upon the hundreds of thousands of memories of that tragic and death-bringing conflict that convulsed our sick planet. Fortunately the story of the *Queen Elizabeth* in World War 2 is one of great success and achievement. It is a happy story in a world that was suffering.

Author Chris Konings was fortunate, indeed, in having the use of a really remarkable series of very fine drawings by the noted Australian-born artist Oswald Brett. Oz Brett served aboard the *Queen Eizabeth*. His talents add tremendously to this fine work. Not only do his sketches show scenes aboard—taking you, for example, right up and into the crows nest—but they depict graphically and with perfect detail many other vessels that the *Queen Elizabeth* passed. The artistic world should hail Chris Konings for bringing Oz Brett's superb World War 2 artwork out of his attic in Levittown, New York!

The scholarly world will praise him for his painstaking and scholarly research into an important chapter in the maritime past. The steamship historian, in particular, will salute him for his recording for posterity the full story of a great ship's war service.

My gratitude for this work also goes to Patrick Stephens, the man and the company, for publishing the volume. Sitting in my study in Sea Cliff as I write this short foreword I am filled with a sense of anticipation for the completed book. It will certainly find a place of honour on my bookshelf and on the shelves of every other lover of the sea and of ships!

Frank O. Braynard
Sea Cliff, NY

Chapter 1

Called up for war

It all started so beautifully in 1936. The Cunard Board of Directors announced that they were intending to start a ferry service across the North Atlantic with two vessels, which were to be the largest liners in the world. The sisters were to sail east or west every week and they would maintain an average speed of 28½ knots to cope with their schedule.

The first of the two was the *Queen Mary*—a miracle in marine development. She became a great success in a short time and the building of her sister was eagerly awaited. Already, before the completion of the *Queen Mary*, Cunard had announced a little about her sister ship—though this was 'still of a preliminary character.' It was not expected that a decision would be made immediately and it was not until the day the *Queen Mary* sailed for New York for the first time, that Sir Percy Bates, Chairman of Cunard, told his naval architects to start on the second vessel.

One of the first changes in the design of the second ship were the funnels. The *Queen Mary* was a three-funnelled ship, but the new liner would only have two and would also 'lose' the supporting wires around the funnels, thus giving passengers much more deck-space. Also, a new design of ventilator made it possible not to use the type installed on the *Queen Mary*, which made that ship very identifiable; the second ship's were to be very sleek and hardly noticeable. Whilst the *Queen Mary* had a well-deck forward, the new vessel was to have a flush main-deck which would give her a cleaner appearance and, because of her sharp raked bow, it would be possible to fit a bow anchor.

At the end of July 1936, it was announced that there were no longer formal problems to be solved and that work on the building of the liner could start at John Brown's shipyard at Clydebank, which had built her sister as well. Yard No 552

was expected to be launched in 1938 and her maiden voyage was planned for 1940.

Work progressed as expected, but the world political situation changed dramatically and, because of this, King George VI could not be present on the day of the launching. This was the period of the Munich Crisis, when Prime Minister Neville Chamberlain was flying to Hitler, desperately trying to avert another war. So, on September 27 1938, it was Queen Eizabeth accompanied by the Princesses Elizabeth and Margaret, who travelled to Scotland to launch the ship that would bear her name—in contrast to what had happened to the *Queen Mary*, the name of Yard No 552 was not kept a secret.

The *Queen Elizabeth* almost took to the water too soon for, during a ten-minute break in the ceremony, whilst waiting for peak tide and whilst the Queen and the Princesses talked with officials, a great noise of breaking timbers was heard and the ship started to move. The Queen, however, remained calm and cut the cord on which the bottle of wine was connected, still in time to name the ship and to see the bottle breaking on the bows.

The *Queen Elizabeth* was on her way to a tremendous task!

War became inevitable and dangerously near, but work was still carried out according to the normal routine. August 23 1939 was annouced as the day that the King and Queen would come and visit the ship's engine-room and third-class accommodation, whilst April 24 1940, would be the day of her maiden voyage. However, all these plans were brought to an abrupt end on the morning of Monday, September 4 1939. When the workers of John Brown's left their work the previous Saturday, the great liner was beautifully painted in her Cunard colours, her funnels distinctively towering above her decks. On that Monday morning she was painted a dullish grey.

Bookings for the maiden voyage were cancelled and many people wondered what would happen to the ship now that Great Britain was at war with Germany, since the latter had so ruthlessly invaded Poland on August 31. Obviously, she would be a sitting target for any German bomber should she remain in the fitting-out basin at the Clyde, but without her interior fitted out properly and without her navigational aids, she could not go very far. For the Germans there could not be a greater propaganda coup than destroying her. Moving her was essential since the space she occupied was urgently wanted for the fitting out of the battleship *Duke Of York,* which had been launched earlier in August. On November 2, the long-awaited licences for the materials to finish the work necessary to move her out of the fitting-out basin were granted by the Ministry of Shipping.

Meanwhile, her engine-room was fitted out and on Friday, December 29 1939, the engines were turned under steam for the first time. Trials started at about 09:00 hours and continued until 16:00 hours, during which time the oil temperature of all bearings was noted and logged and revolutions noted at various steam pressures. Later, tests were made of the emergency equipment fitted to the main engines against the event of any failure of auxiliary equipment.

Two months later, Cunard received a letter from the Admiralty stating that Mr Churchill, by then First Lord of the Admiralty, wanted the ship to depart from Clydeside as soon as possible and 'to keep away from the British Isles as long as the order was in force'. This caused a spate of company board conferences, on the question of where she was to go.

The number of ports available to the *Queen Elizabeth* was limited and another vital factor was the tide on the Clyde. A ship of this size only has a depth of water sufficient to navigate her to the open sea twice a year, and the first suitable occasion in this case was at the end of February 1940, when there would be two such tides within 24 hours. The first tide had to be used to move her out of the basin, whilst the second was to be used for the *Duke Of York* to go in. The operation had to be successful, for if she were to miss the tide there would not be another chance until six months later .

In the meantime, Cunard had decided to take

her to New York. Her sister ship, *Queen Mary,* had been lying there since September 1939 and now the *Queen Elizabeth* was to join her, though getting her out of the Clyde secretly would not be an easy task.

Apart from being the world's largest liner, it was impossible that local people would not notice her being stored and fuelled. All the other normal procedures to prepare a ship for sailing, and moving her from her basin down the Clyde were certainly something nobody could miss. Therefore a decoy was needed and announcements were made that she was being sent to Southampton where she would go into dry dock for inspection of hull, rudder and propellers. Furniture would be fitted there as well. So, many crates of stores and parts were sent to Southampton and, for those who would sail in her down south, hotel rooms were booked and a crew of 400 was mustered for the voyage. Apparently, the camouflage was successful, because on the day the liner should have arrived in Southampton, the sky was filled with German bombers! Meanwhile, the ship was registered at Custom House, Liverpool, and given her official number 166290 and signal letters GBSS.

Also, as part of her preparation for wartime use, she was fitted out with a degaussing device, which consisted of 10,000 yds of cable encircling the ship, somewhere 40 ft above the water-line, through which powerful electric currents ran, in order to demagnetize the ship so that she would not trigger off magnetic mines. Normally, the power was adjusted when the ship's position towards the Magnetic North and South Poles changed and it was considered that on a depth of over 200 fathoms the currents could be turned off.

The crew arrived on February 22 1940 and on the morning of the 26th the *Queen Elizabeth* left her fitting-out basin, stripped of 24 of her lifeboats, for the removal of every possible ton of weight to lessen her draught was required. Two accident boats remained in their davits. Assisted by tugs

Left *'The Queen' takes to the water, September 27 1938* (Stewart Bale).

Right *Blue card issued to a Cunard engineer on February 26 1940.*

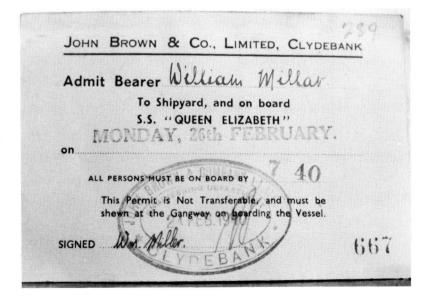

JOHN BROWN & CO., LIMITED, CLYDEBANK

Admit Bearer *William Millar*

To Shipyard, and on board
S.S. "QUEEN ELIZABETH"
MONDAY, 26th FEBRUARY.

on ....

ALL PERSONS MUST BE ON BOARD BY 40

This Permit is Not Transferable, and must be shewn at the Gangway on boarding the Vessel.

SIGNED *Wm. Millar.*

667

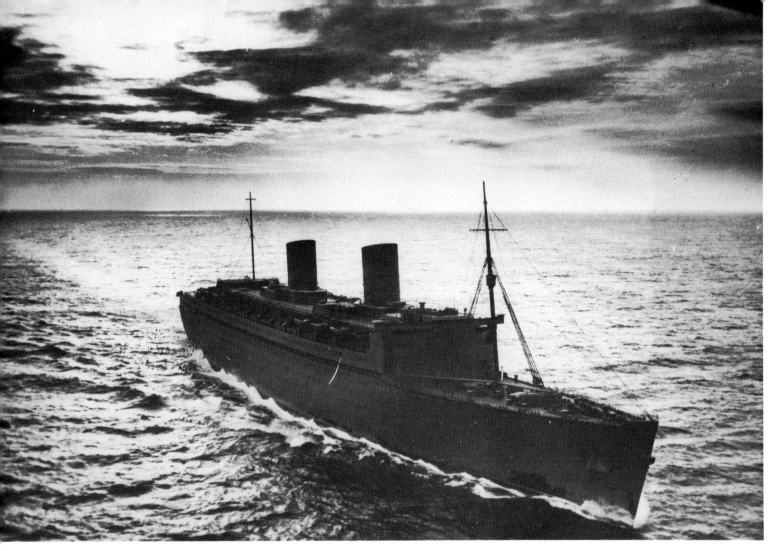

Above left *The tricky passage downstream to Tail-of-the-Bank* (The Times).
Below left *February 26 1940. The first move—a 'Lady' prepares for war* (The Times).
Above *March 7 1940. The first glimpse of the* Queen Elizabeth *off Fire Island on her dash to New York* (Holland Fotobureau).

and at first watched by only a few people, the world's largest liner, in her dull grey coat, slowly moved down the river and, at virtually the same spot her sister had gone aground, she was caught by the incoming tide, taking the stern tugs almost an hour to get control of her. By that time the banks of the river had become crowded and all work in other shipyards and factories had stopped, as workers left to watch the ship go by. After five hours, she finally anchored off Tail-of-the-Bank, which later, though no one would have thought it at the time, would become one of her major wartime ports.

The following day, the *Queen Elizabeth* was handed over to the Cunard Company and the crew were told that the liner was going to make an ocean voyage, the destination unknown. Those who did not want to join the ship on this trip were given a chance to leave, whilst others had to sign on again, for a different set of articles was now required, changed from coastal to foreign.

As sailing day drew near, final inspections were carried out, as well as wireless tests and engine and compass trials. Then, at seven o'clock on the morning of March 2 1940, the King's Messenger arrived with a sealed envelope. Captain Townley knew that this envelope was not to be opened till she was well at sea, when he would know that she was bound for New York. Thirty minutes later, filled with 6,000 tons of oil, unarmed and escorted by four destroyers and some aircraft, the *Queen Elizabeth* slipped away from the misty Clyde. Tow hundred miles west of Rathlin Island, the destroyers turned back, leaving the ship on her own, wishing her 'Good Luck—Bon Voyage'.

During the voyage, Captin Townley had to maintain a strict radio silence. If in any circumstances the ship would have to avoid a convoy or a German submarine, the Royal Navy would contact her. The only defence she had was her speed and manoeuvrability, though at this stage these depended on figures rather than on facts. Inside, the ship was far from completed. There were no carpets and miles of unconnected wiring dangled all over her. Also, the ship was very cold, for no heating had been installed yet, but her engines and boilers were running splendidly and she ploughed through the sea at an

Above left *Another pilot's eye-view off Fire Island* (Imperial War Museum).
Left *Gee! But she's* big (Mariner's Museum, Newport News, Virginia).
Above *Down anchor. First stop Quarantine Base* (Holland Fotobureau).

Above left *First view for New York Port officials at Quarantine Base* (Mariner's Museum, Newport News, Virginia).
Below left *A great skyline welcomes a great 'Lady' to Pier 90 for the first time* (Imperial War Museum).
Above *Approaching her berth at Pier 90, showing some signs of 'wear in her make-up'.*

average speed of 26 knots. Meanwhile, in New York, people were making arrangements to receive the ship at Pier 90, again under strict secrecy. The *Mauretania* was tied up there and the arrival of the *Queen Elizabeth* meant she had to be moved.

On the *Queen Elizabeth* a daily routine developed. The Staff Captain would make his round of inspection, whilst the technicians, on board from the time she left the Clyde, inspected her machinery and equipment. Sometimes people made a walk around the decks and, in doing so, some of them got the impression they were on a ghost ship. Everything was so empty that in the dining-rooms one could hear one's echo when speaking and corridors were no more than miles

of deserted alley-ways. Light was from exposed bulbs hanging on their wires and, throughout the night, a complete blackout was in force for those areas which led to open decks.

Though hardly a luxury voyage, the people on this maiden voyage enjoyed themselves in various ways. One of these was the very good and varied food prepared for her complement of passengers. Every day their menu was printed in the printing shop, which also providing the membership cards to the 'Unruffled Elizabethans' Club,' formed during the voyage in the Purser's office, and consisting of those '. . . on the combined trial trip and maiden voyage of HMS *Queen Elizabeth*, leaving Glasgow for New York on February 26, 1940. On account of wartime conditions the plaudits of the public were replaced by a providential mist and an escort of HM destroyers and seaplanes.' The club's object was 'to establish the proposition that true Twentieth-century Elizabethans are able to remain under all conditions completely unruffled'! Club members amused themselves with discussions, by telling stories or by giving performances on musical instruments during the evening hours.

Dashing across the ocean and still zig-zagging, the *Queen Elizabeth* was first spotted by the crew of an aeroplane on March 7 1940, some 40 miles east of Fire Island. Rust spots were visible, now that the paint had started to peel off. The aircraft's crew reported that only a few lifeboats were carried and that the ship was riding high out of the water. They could not read her name as the whole ship was painted grey, while her silhouette was unknown. The only thing they thought was that the ship was in danger and seeking shelter—most likely in New York.

The *Queen Elizabeth* anchored off Quarantine Base first, before proceeding up the Hudson on the next tide. Her welcome in New York was tremendous. Thousands of people watched her sliding by and every ship in the harbour gave her a whistle welcome, which was answered by her own deep siren. Ticker-tape whirled from the skyscrapers and offices and, as she passed the *Queen Mary*, the two ships saluted each other by dipping their Red Ensigns.

The evening papers had already announced the liner's arrival in their headlines and remarked that those New Yorkers, who had gone out to see her sailing by, would have had an ever-memorable view of the ship to pass on to their children.

The *New York Times* wrote in March 1940: 'The world has come to expect naval feats of the British, but there is a quality of sharp suprise and almost mischievous daring about the *Queen Elizabeth's* first voyage that electrifies the pulse. The British can take well justified satisfaction in an opportunity so courageously seized and so adroitly carried out. Many sagas of the sea have begun and ended in our harbour, but can the old-timers remember anything to compare with the unheralded arrival of the biggest and fastest liner in the world, after the most daring of all maiden crossings? It did not matter that the *Queen Elizabeth* wore a drab coat of grey on her first visit

Three of a kind in good company (postcard, Chris Konings collection).

THE THREE BIGGEST SHIPS IN THE WORLD, WAR REFUGEES IN NEW YORK   (12)

QUEEN ELIZABETH (at right)   QUEEN MARY (center)   NORMANDIE (at left)

Gross Tonnage: 85,000   Gross Tonnage: 81,000   Gross Tonnage: 83,000

Shifted to the south side of Pier 90 and awaiting further orders (Steamship Historical Society of America).

to New York or that no bands went down the bay to meet her. The interest of New Yorkers was echoed by the admiration of Americans for those who built her, sailed her and sent her on her way.

'Any landlubber can see that the *Queen Elizabeth* is a fine ship, as sleek and graceful as a yacht; a credit to the British Merchant Marine. Her distinction is not only in being the largest ship in the world; she is also new in design, as the *Queen Mary* was not. The *Queen Mary* was planned before the crossing of the *Bremen*, the *Rex* and the *Normandie*. The *Queen Elizabeth* is the first superliner to embody the lessons of these maritime pioneers of our streamlined era. The British were right in not leaving such a ship at the mercy of air attack at home. Their luxury liners will have a job to do when the war is over. The dramatic maiden voyage of the *Queen Elizabeth* proves that the British are looking ahead to the days of peace and to the laurels of peace which must be won . . .'

Once alongside the pier, the ship remained sealed and only official visitors were allowed to go up the gangway. Port officials could only come aboard under escort and by no means was there to be any publicity or the taking of photographs. Cunard's statement to the press was simple: 'In

view of the circumstances, it was decided that the *Queen Elizabeth* should proceed to America, which she did, leaving last Saturday and arriving today, after an uneventful voyage at a moderate speed. No attempt at an unusually high speed was made. The ship carried no passengers or cargo. The interior accomodation is not wholly completed. No plans have been made for the vessel beyond tying her up at Pier 90, alongside the *Queen Mary*, in line with the arrangements in effect for all ships of the Company stopping at American Ports. No visitors will be allowed on the Pier or the ship during the present stay in New York . . . '

A fortnight after this glorious saga had ended in New York, the *Queen Mary* left America for Sydney, to start a career as a troop-ship, and it soon became apparent that this would happen to the *Queen Elizabeth* as well. However, it was not until September that the decision was made that she had to follow her sister. This time she would not be as bare as on her first voyage for, whilst in New York, her fitting out as a passenger liner was taken up again and she received lighting, heating, ventilation, telephones, water and sanitary services, lifts etc. Although still not yet properly fitted out, she was to sail early in November.

Chapter 2

The Suez Shuttle

And so the *Queen Elizabeth* left New York, on that wet morning of November 13, for her new destination, Singapore. There, she had to go into dry dock prior to going to Sydney, where she was to be refitted as a troop-ship. On board were a few company experts who would control the conversion works, of which a part were to be done in Singapore docks as well. Still painted in battleship grey and unarmed, she first headed for Trinidad and Cape Town—two ports that had the facilities to supply her with fuel and water, for her limited endurance of 6,000 miles did not allow her to make the voyage in one long haul. The visit to Cape Town caused some excitement there and many people went out to get a glimpse of the liner anchored off Table Bay. At first it was thought that she was the *Mauretania*, which had anchored there previously but as soon as the news spread that she was the *Queen Elizabeth*, people became very anxious to see her. She did not get a real welcome on arrival in Singapore Naval Docks, however. The *Queen Mary* had been there shortly before and some of the *Mary's* crew members had caused trouble when enjoying Singapore's nightlife.

In the Naval Docks she was fitted with her heavy 6-in gun mounted on a 1908 platform on the after mooring deck, as well as 3-in AA guns, one on either quarter at the after ends of the promenade deck and another amidships, just abaft the 'verandah grill', which was a slightly raised section of the boat deck aft. The *Queen Elizabeth*, now with a black-painted hull and grey upper-works, left Singapore for Fremantle on February 11 escorted by HMS *Durban*, after an eight days' spell in the docks where security had been very bad. With a short stop of two days at Fremantle to refuel and water (15—17 February), she routed south of Tasmania unescorted, with a speed of 25 knots, to arrive in Sydney for the first time on the February 21 1941.

Crowds of people lined the famous North and South Heads, some with their cameras to take pictures of the magnificent ship and others to get a glimpse of her. It looked as if half the population of Sydney had taken a day off to watch her entering port and all seemed to know somehow that she was coming. The famous Sydney Harbour Bridge was crowded and everywhere you could see people using binoculars so as not to miss a second of the spectacle. Many harbour ferries were loaded to the gunwales with people and some of them listed dangerously when passing the liner.

Australians had always been very proud of their harbour and it was a dent in this pride to realise that there was not enough room to have the two *Queens* in port at the same time. The *Queen Elizabeth* needed a minimum of 1,100 ft to moor and another 1,100 for swinging on the tides. Lying at anchor off Bradley's Head was the only place where she could swing and not block harbour traffic. So, here she was anchored at Athol Bight, and when the wind suddenly blew from the south in a southerly bluster, usually after a spell of hot weather, it would catch the *Queen Elizabeth* broad on the starboard beam. She would heel right over and only gradually right herself as she swung round and pointed up to her anchor cable, facing the south. This was a fascinating sight to watch and, of course, the *Elizabeth* became a major attraction for the people of Sydney.

Soon, all sorts of traffic became a common sight around her, bringing various kinds of material to fit her out as a troop-ship and taking back ashore some of her furniture (mainly cabin beds) to be stored in Sydney. The Cockatoo Docks and Engineering Company completed this work in a few weeks. Australian troops were badly needed in Africa and, within a short time, the *Queen Elizabeth* had to sail with double her normal

passenger capacity. Bunks to carry more than 5,000 men were fitted. The first class dining room became the troops' mess hall, whilst the tourist class dining room was used as the officers' mess room. Navigating officers also ate there but engineering officers had their own mess rooms. However, despite the fact that the *Queen Elizabeth* now carried double the number of her peacetime passenger complement, the Australians were still able to use the theatre and swimming pools in the normal way.

Dr Maguire, the ship's doctor, started to prepare adequate hospital accommodation. He changed the dance salon into the main ward and other wards were fitted up in the smoke room and garden lounges. He also thought of the badly injured and placed an isolation hospital at the aft end of the ship. As the *Queen Elizabeth* did not have stabilisers, Dr Maguire insisted that the hospital beds be placed athwartships, to help the patients feel more comfortable when the ship was rolling heavily. Also, an X-ray apparatus, loaned by the Australian Red Cross, was installed in the turkish bath.

Much of what had been done in Singapore was done again by the Australians and, when this work was finished, the *Queen Elizabeth* left Sydney for Hobart, Tasmania, on April 1 1941. Her visit to Hobart was undertaken so that the *Queen Mary* could come in to Sydney to pick up her load of troops.

The *Queen Mary* left on the 9th for Jervis Bay, to make place for her companion. After a two-day spell in Sydney, the *Queen Elizabeth* sailed on April 11 1941, having embarked her first load of Australian troops for the Middle East. On board were 5,333 soldiers, consisting of army, air force and naval personnel, who were taken to the ship from Circular Quay by a ferry which made fast alongside the *Queen Elizabeth*. There was a stairway up to the shell door. There was also a boat from Man-o-War Steps, around from Sydney Cove, to which naval boats brought the Admirals and the other naval staff based at Garden Island. The troops were given tickets stating the number

A Royal Occasion! Two 'Queens' meet for the first time at sea, off Sydney Heads whilst exchanging berths between Jervis Bay and Athol Bay, NSW, April 9 1941 (National Library of Australia).

of their berth and mealtimes, and some of them were marched round and round the endless passage-ways. It is no surprise that they lost all sense of direction, for most of them had never been on such a ship before, and even crew members found the size of the ship most impressive.

Since she was built for the North Atlantic, she did not have any air-conditioning facilities at all, so most of the time it was 'as hot as Hades'—and what ventilation there was proved completely ineffective. Tempers rose, though after a few futile attempts at roll-call and a lot of angry talk between officers and men ('cattle on a freight train got more room than we did', a trooper recalls), the passengers resigned to this being 'home' and started to settle in. With this number of men on board, the ship seemed to be very crowded and troops felt they did not have an inch of room, especially as the hammocks were slung so close together that each touched the next.

All cameras had been registered and photography was forbidden, but some took a few furtive shots. It was even possible to take some pictures of the decks when looking at the crowds in boats circling around searching for friends and relatives on board. Although the Sydney authorities had done their utmost to keep the movements of the *Queen Elizabeth* a secret, a vessel of her size was very difficult to hide and, of course, the movement of troops on all these ferries meant that interest in the ship grew. Eventually, on this, the first sailing from Sydney, security went overboard completely. Everything that could more or less safely keep afloat was chartered and hired to carry well-wishers and spectators out to the ship and there were even special excursions to the ship, from which many of the troops threw farewell notes to the crowds.

It was a question of some interest to the crew, whether she would come up to expectations on this trip. She would sail in convoy with the *Queen Mary, Mauretania, Nieuw Amsterdam* and the *Ile de France,* ships which had already sailed on several trooping voyages and had encountered great difficulties and some exciting moments. The *Queen Elizabeth* was very much the junior vessel, with a new and inexperienced crew.

The *Mauretania* and *Nieuw Amsterdam,* carrying New Zealand troops, had both arrived at Sydney on April 10, under a heavy escort, and the *Ile de France* had taken on Australians at Melbourne. The *Queen Elizabeth* was to join the other three and after that they would rendezvous with the *Mary* at Jervis Bay.

A channel was (mine) swept in the Bass Strait

April 1941. Queen Elizabeth, *leaving Sydney for the first time, loaded with Commonwealth troops. Pleasure craft swarming around bid their fond farewells* (Australian War Memorial, NH 1471).

Convoy US 10 passing through Bass Strait—a mighty collection of transport vessels: far left, Nieuw Amsterdam; *foreground,* HMT Queen Mary; *centre right,* HMT Queen Elizabeth; *far right,* HMT Mauretania; Ile de France, *not shown on picture, probably lies further astern* (Stewart Bale).

for the passage of US10 (codename for the convoy). As anti-submarine protection on leaving Sydney, and for the *Queen Mary* at Jervis Bay, as far as circumstances permitted, air patrols were provided, as well as for the south-east area. An auxiliary minesweeper was to be stationed at the centre of the entrance to the swept channel at Fremantle, prior to the convoy's arrival there. In Fremantle, water and fuel were to be taken on, an operation which was to be handled at Gage Roads, one mile off the North Mole. Up to Fremantle, US10 was to be escorted by HMAS *Australia* but from there the convoy would split up. *Nieuw Amsterdam, Mauretania* and the *Ile de France* were going to Colombo, whilst the two *Queens* would proceed to Trincomalee, escorted by HMAS *Canberra*, now under the codename US10A.

During the trip to Fremantle, the troops on board had the time to get used to the ship, though many of them still had difficulties in locating their berths again. Lunches were served in the spacious dining room and the food was good. Everyone seemed glad to be aboard at last and did not even seem to mind the canteen being dry. Some of the troops hated to do the necessary jobs, such as sweeping, washing up and mess orderly services. Life was quite heavily organised and, as one weary soul commented, life was an 'endless round of PT parades, boat parades, equipment parades, "dick" parades and God knows what other kind of parades . . . !' So, it became a matter of either becoming 'seasick' for a while or changing one's attitude to all the chores.

A mess orderly recalls 'At mealtimes there were three sittings at twenty minute intervals—140 tables in a room, which was a grand affair though hardly one's idea of pleasant dining. The room itself was too heavily ornate, with insufficient air and light. At each sitting the drill seemed to be that we line up to get meat, bread, etc, yelling out our table number as we do so. Then we cleared away and washed and re-set the tables. It was as hot as buggery working there and you steamed

with perspiration, but never mind—we all worked fast and well and got the job done quickly, so we could get out of there and up to some clean, fresh air. Doing this job we didn't have to attend any sort of parade, except for boat drill, which was compulsory for all, so maybe mess orderly wasn't too bad a job after all . . .!' He estimated the population on board to be 1,658,830 per square mile!

Two-up, cards and Crown-and-Anchor passed the time of day. Sometimes about twenty different games were going on in the bar and at one time one big group of players needed so much room that nobody else could get in. There was constant yelling and smoke, the fetid air became quite nauseous—moreover the atmosphere did not improve as the ship headed for Suez. With the ever increasing temperature on board, the canteen had a busy time in selling beer, resulting in many drunks aboard, spitting and spewing, singing and general disorderliness. Some men were so drunk that they took their showers fully dressed and then went straight to bed. The stifling heat below made tempers very short; speaking out of turn became physically hazardous! The ventilators were definitely inadequate and the heat sapped the men's vitality. There was little for them to do, but read, gamble or argue but at least the sea was calm.

For quite a number of these 'diggers', Trincomalee came as a welcome change, on April 26 1941. It only took the *Elizabeth* half a day to take in fuel and water before sailing on to Suez, escorted by HMAS *Canberra*, at a speed of 25 knots. *Queen Mary* was to follow and rejoin the convoy one day later and both vessels would then proceed for the Red Sea.

On April 28 a distress call was received from *Clan Buchanan* in a position about 330 miles to port of the convoy. That ship was sunk by the *Penguin* and the *Canberra* was ordered to remain with the convoy. Also, reports came in that mines had been sighted in the southern Red Sea, near the convoy's route, for which extra protection was provided with the ship's paravanes.

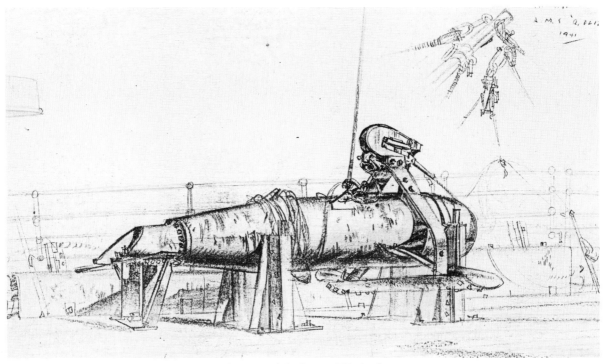

Port paravane, stowed at the after-end of the foredeck of the Queen Elizabeth.

The paravanes were stowed on the after end of the foredeck and were only used in shallow waters. They were used to locate and cut mines from their underwater points of suspension, so that they would float to the surface, where they would be destroyed by machine gun fire—sometimes a dangerous operation. The paravanes transmitted a loud, monotonous hum to the wires towing them, which echoed and reverberated in the hull in the forepart of the vessel. Their wires frequently snapped, in which case the ship would be unable to pick them up again, because of the mines around her. The convoy streamed the paravanes until reaching Perim Island, where *Canberra* left for Aden and speed was increased to 27 knots.

Port Tewfik, situated about two miles from the southern end of the Suez Canal, suffered from the same difficulties as Sydney. The port could only handle one of the *Queens* at a time, so the *Queen Mary* went up first at full speed,whilst the *Queen Elizabeth* had to sail along behind her under the ever pitiless sun. Because of the Italian defeat in Eritrea, the ships could go all the way from Aden to Suez unescorted. The southern part of the Red Sea was fairly free of danger. It was hot, however, and this caused many problems associated with drink. Beer was rationed to one pint per man, per day—and that only with an officer's

permission—which sometimes caused a mutinous feeling among the troops. This seldom came to anything serious, apart from the occasional fights with food and plates.

The canteen closed until the end of the trip, and lifebelts were to be worn continuously until the ship reached her destination. With the weather very hot and the sea deadly calm, the troops all wanted to go ashore now—no matter what the place was called or who was there.

Moving up to Port Tewfik, the Red Sea became dangerous. The Adabeiah Mole was the only place which could receive the troops and there was no real anti-aircraft protection, apart from a crack AA Cruiser and the Germans were very close. There was always an extra look-out for aircraft alarm and most of the time the troopships would leave Port Tewfik after dark, because of Luftwaffe Alarm, sailing approximately 180 miles during which they spent several hours out of danger, to arrive back again the following morning.

During the time between dawn and dusk the *Queen Elizabeth* lay at anchor, disembarking troops and embarking Italian or German POWs, as well as wounded soldiers all handled by Nile barges owned by Egyptians. Because of the fact that the Luftwaffe was able to reach Port Tewfik from Alexandria, at any moment of the day, (dis)embarking operations needed to be handled FAST. The *Queen Elizabeth* was a sitting duck for German bombers which were kept informed of ship's position by high flying spotter planes.

This first time in the Red Sea she stayed for three days before leaving again for Singapore on May 6 1941, this time without any POWs or wounded, for she needed dry docking—first for cleaning of the ship's bottom and then for engine overhaul. Being a new ship, her engines were not yet run in and it was essential that they should be checked before proceeding to Sydney again. Following this she would make three round voyages to the Middle East—the first in convoy with the *Aquitania* and the *Queen Mary*, and the second with the *Queen Mary* escorted by HMS *Cornwall*.

The policy usually followed was to keep the convoy darkened and without navigation lights at night. All portholes and doors were closed and no smoking on the upper decks was allowed after dark. It was sometimes amusing to see that other ships, like the *Ile de France*, were belching flames from their funnels which could be seen for miles.

Right *Entering dry dock at Singapore, May 1941, for major overhaul* (Imperial War Museum).
Below *October 25 1941.* Queen Elizabeth *visits Hobart, Tasmania.*

Only when it was necessary to avoid other ships at close quarters were the navigation lights lit. This led to two fairly narrow escapes from collision with darkened ships while passing through routes south-east and south of Ceylon and the policy was then changed. *Cornwall* burned dimmed navigation lights for the rest of the time in this area, which resulted in two darkened and otherwise invisible ships which might have endangered the convoy, switching on their lights until clear. However, if visibility fell below three miles all ships showed their lights.

After this event, the Captain on board HMS *Cornwall* asked whether this policy was to be applied to both fast and slow convoys, bearing in mind that the enemy was fitted with radio direction finders, as it was believed all German warships were, there was little secrecy of movement to be gained by always having ships darkened at night, especially in areas where friendly shipping, moving darkened, was likely to prove a navigational danger.

Her last trip to the Middle East started with a short visit to Hobart where she arrived early in the afternoon of October 25 1941. This was a

pleasant time for the crew, who were entertained by the islanders arranging drives and dances. The visit to Tasmania really lifted the morale of the crew. Many of them had felt like invisible ghosts in a ship completely blocked from communication with the outside world. It was greatly appreciated that some people knew something about their work and the tensions on the ship. After a spell of some six days she left for Sydney on November 1. She arrived there one day later, to embark about 4,500 troops, whilst the *Queen Mary* waited for her at Jervis Bay. When the *Queen Elizabeth* set off to join the *Queen Mary* she received the same tremendous farewell that she had received on the previous occasions and thousands of people were again along the shore in anticipation of the ship leaving the harbour.

On November 3, the two ships headed for Fremantle, under escort of the *Canberra* again. From there the convoy was to meet HMS *Cornwall* somewhere in the midst of the Indian Ocean on the way to Trincomalee after which *Canberra* would return to Australia.

Then, right in the middle of that vast expanse of water something spectacular happened. On the

notice-board there appeared a message to the effect that mail would be collected in the afternoon. Mail was always eagerly awaited and of course the writing of letters was very popular since that was the only way of communicating with relatives back home about the trip, after censorship, of course. The question that remained was how this mail collection would be effected—for there were no helicopters as we have today and no mailship was in evidence. The solution was quite simple—but quite breathtaking! The escort *Canberra* moving at full speed lowered a pinnace which cruised towards the two huge liners now both hove to (sitting ducks for any submarine!). When the pinnace had collected bags of mail from each *Queen* she was hoisted in again and the cruiser left for Australia. HMS *Cornwall* immediately proceeded for Trincomalee in escort with the two vessels, coded Convoy US13.

Fascinating moments—for, just a few days prior to this event, the cruiser HMAS *Sydney* was sunk by the German *Kormoran* not far from the place the *Queens* stopped, and lost without survivors. The German ship played dumb, however, and insisted that she was the *Straat Malakka*, a Dutch vessel, and kept jumbling the signals. It was rumoured that HMS *Cornwall* had sunk the *Kormoran*, but this was untrue, although it may have been that she was seeking that particular German ship.

As on other voyages through the Indian Ocean, the ship rolled heavily again. Spilled tea and slops made the floor like a greased glacier and some of the troops took advantage of the ship's roll doing long-distance slides. Most of them, however, were really sick and, for them, Trincomalee made a welcome change again in this tedious and boring existence. Many went out and looked at the beautiful scenery afforded by the harbour, set amongst islands and headlands of luxuriant jungle, verdant greens and rich beauty. Some fields of soft new green were visible—tea plantations—and also a few fishing boats. Coppers were thrown to the natives, though no bumboats were allowed around the ship and so there was very little other enterainment—but, to be at tropical Tricomalee was exciting enough. The troops were allowed to send a cable home,

Left *A well deserved rest in Hobart. Note how her size dominates the harbour.*
Above *The* Queen Mary *in the Indian Ocean, as seen from a shell door on board the* Queen Elizabeth, *in convoy bound to the Middle East with Australian troops. November 1941.*
Right Queen Elizabeth's *funnels from a lifeboat. Starboard, looking forward, bound towards Sydney from Port Tewfik, Egypt, on the last voyage to the Middle East from Australia. Unfinished sketch, November 1941.*

Queen Elizabeth *arriving at Port Tewfik, Egypt, with the last detachment of Australian troops for the Middle East. Sunrise, Monday, November 24 1941. RIN Sloop* Sutlej *in foreground* (from a painting by Oswald Brett, 1977).

selecting a few standard numbered phrases from a list. For example, 34, 46 or 72 would mean 'Fondest Love: Good Luck and Best Health: Are you all right?'

During the morning of November 15, HMS *Cornwall* carried out sub-calibre firings and exercising breakdowns off Trincomalee, after which she sailed with the convoy again to Suez. As on every trip, the convoy carried out HA (high angle) firings. These were performed with the aid of a target kite, towed by the cruiser. HMS *Cornwall* left the convoy on the 20th and the two ships proceeded into the Red Sea where they arrived four days later. Again, one *Queen* went to Suez, whilst the other one reduced speed and waited.

After disembarking the Aussie troops, the *Queen Elizabeth* embarked another batch of POWs and wounded. A German POW recalls: 'We were transferred from *Lager Hellian* to the Suez Canal borders by motor vehicle. Without any sort of stop, we had to sit in full daylight with a burning sun on our head. Point of embarkation was *Punkt Rotes Meer*. The majestic sight of the ship was something we will never forget, and this was emphasised by the blue water and again that burning sun. One other thing that impressed us a lot was the fact that we could see the ship's propellers through the clear water. Everything went very quiet. There was no rush in getting on board and we all were treated strictly by the rules of the Geneva Convention. There was no idea of

any sort of retaliation towards us and most of us were well impressed by "The Englische Lords". Barbed wire was only there when it was needed as a sort of blockade, but certainly by no means to limit personal freedom, and since there was a War on and forms of limiting personal freedom could vary a lot, this could hardly be called one.' Some of the POWs were really amazed by their first sight of Sydney and of course the famous Sydney Harbour Bridge, and most Australian people were very impressive to them as well. Though there was no reason for them to be hungry, they were overwhelmed with food. Bread, fruit and cigarettes were handed to the Germans, and that was something they never expected.

By the time the *Queen Elizabeth* arrived back in Sydney on December 16, the world situation had changed dramatically. On Sunday, December 7 1941, the American naval base at Pearl Harbor was attacked by six Japanese aircraft carriers, which had launched two large waves of bombers. Within a short time the major units of the American Pacific Fleet were destroyed or immobilised. Everything was carried out without a declaration of war, and it was because of this surprise attack that the Americans lost many of their ships. Fortunately, two of their aircraft carriers, the US *Enterprise* and *Lexington*, were at sea together with several cruisers and destroyers and remained unscathed.

Now America was at war and the two *Queens* were badly needed for transporting US reinforcements to Australia, for combat in the Pacific theatre, and these ships were the quickest available to get them there. Also the safety of the *Queen Elizabeth* in Australian waters began to cause some anxiety. Referring to her limited range and her fuel consumption, it was pointed out that the only refuge ports were Sydney (where only one *Queen* could berth) and Hobart, where anti-submarine defence could not be provided for an extended period. The use of Fremantle was not considered suitable owing to the difficulty of anti-submarine defence of Gage Roads, where the *Queen Elizabeth* had to anchor. This port could not be omitted altogether without reducing reserves to an undesirably small limit and, with the war in the Far East expanding, it was now thought that reinforcements to the Middle East were better lifted by ships which could berth alongside at Fremantle and which had a far more extensive and economical range, while the *Queens* could be used to ferry American forces across the Pacific.

Chapter 3

Pacific Passage

The *Queen Mary* had already headed for the Clyde, prior to going to New York and picking up her first load of American troops. The *Queen Elizabeth* now had to cross the Pacific, to San Francisco, to pick up her's, but before that, she badly needed dry docking and by now the number of dry docks that could handle her had been cut down to four. She was sent to Esquimalt, in British Columbia, Canada, for Southampton suffered from heavy German bombing, as did Singapore from the Japanese, and the last possibility, Boston, USA, was busy at this time.

Sending her to the other end of the world needed tremendous organisation, for the *Queen Elizabeth* could not make the run in one haul and, even at the slow, economic cruising speed of 21 knots, which was undoubtedly necessary, there was still much danger for, although these liners were sometimes heavily armed, enemy submarines could still break through. Air attacks could also be expected, and, despite her armament, the *Queen Elizabeth* would be a prize objective for them.

For weeks she lay in Sydney harbour while she was fitted with two concrete mounts on the foredeck scuttle, in which two 3-in guns would be placed in Esquimalt. Previous to this, shortly before she left Port Tewfik, she had been fitted with two Oerlikons. The threat of attack was definitely serious! All of these heavier guns were relics from the First World War but the ship's crew were also trained to handle some of the lighter Vickers machine-guns. They were made familiar with the guns during their stay in Sydney and the 3-in ammunition seemed to be more dangerous to the crew than to any enemy aircraft. The Garden Island naval Petty Officer who instructed the crew told them, in the event of a misfire, to remove the shell (it could explode at any moment) and dump it over the side FAST!

Then, on February 6, she departed from Sydney with a first stop, on the morning of February 8, at Auckland, New Zealand. Here she was trimmed to the tops with fuel and water, before heading for the Pacific. Some clever crew members even filled their bath tubs with fresh water as well. Two days later she left Auckland; soon after when streaming the paravanes, one of the devices hit a wreck, damaging 100 ft of rail along the foc'sle and losing the paravane davit as well. However, this was a small accident as she started her dash across that perfidious ocean and what an effect the change to 21 knots had on the crew! Used to 7½ knots more, they had felt pretty safe on board this fast vessel, but now they realised what would have happened if she had been torpedoed in the midst of the Indian Ocean with a few thousand troops on board. Of course, there were the lifeboats and rafts, but what use would they have been if there were any panic?

Fortunately, she arrived safely at Nuku Hiva, on the Marquesas Islands, rendezvousing secretly

Queen Elizabeth *passing North Head on her way to Esquimalt, BC, February 6 1942* (National Library of Australia).

Above Queen Elizabeth *at sea on her way to Esquimalt, BC. Note machine-gun on scuttle and protective bridge shield.*
Below *Anchored in Royal Roads, BC, waiting for the tide to take her into Esquimalt. Note escort vessels in the background, February 23 1942* (Public Archives, Canada).
Above right *Entering dry-dock, Esquimalt, BC, 1942* (Public Archives, Canada).
Below right *All fast! Dock emptied! Work to get her back into shape again is begun. Note the preliminary works on hull to change the position of the degaussing gear* (Public Archives, Canada).

with a tanker to refuel. When sailing through the narrow entrance, the ship's crew looked eagerly to see if the tanker was there, but nothing was to be seen. In fact, there was hardly any sign of life, only a few crabs. The beauty of the island, with its green jungle, made the atmosphere change—it was as if the ship were trapped. It seemed as if she was surrounded by trees, with no possible escape left. The *Queen Elizabeth* whistled, a pre-arranged signal, but nothing was heard, only her echo.

A few natives came running to the shore and quickly vanished again. It must have been quite a shock to them, to see such a great monster arrive on their shores when in the past they had only seen an occasional schooner. They were obviously very curious—but so were the crew!

Radio-silence had not been broken on the way from Auckland and no one could tell what might have happened to that very important tanker. However, immense relief was obvious when, after

ten minutes, the naval tanker *Bishopdale* slowly rounded the headland. This was a most remarkable occasion, for the two vessels had been directed and navigated from opposite ends of the earth to meet at this specific time, on this tiny island, right in the middle of nowhere.

One of the *Queen Elizabeth's* deck officers couldn't stem his emotions when he expressed with feeling, 'What the hell's kept you?' It relieved a lot of tension on the *Queen* but it also caused anger amongst some of the tanker crew. It had been a long and arduous journey, carrying such a hazardous cargo and, to top it all, she had run out of many provisions and all the flour on board had gone sour! However, good humour was restored when one enterprising Australian sailor went ashore and returned in a canoe loaded with fruit. However, once on board, the fruit was destroyed and he was bathed in Phenol, antiseptics and many different kinds of detergents to decontaminate him. On this trip there was no shore leave and he was severely punished. Having exchanged various stores with the tanker, the *Queen Elizabeth* left for Esquimalt, just twelve hours after her arrival in the Marquesas Islands. This time, at full speed, it took her just a little more than a week to cross and reach the Canadian port.

At Esquimalt, port and naval officers had been busy organising her arrival. The depth of Esquimalt harbour did not permit the *Queen Elizabeth* to lie alongside or at anchor and so extensive dredging operations were carried out. Even then she had to arrive at the peak of the tide as light as possible to get her 39ft draught into dry dock which showed only 38 ft over the sill at high water. A block-plan of the ship and docking plans were flown over from England and to provide sufficient tugs, two were borrowed from the 13th Naval District in Seattle. Ministry of War Transport representatives supervised all works. She picked up the pilot on the morning of February 23 1942.

Escorted by five corvettes up the Sound and with planes flying overhead she dropped anchor to wait for the right tide. A heavy snowstorm made it even worse that day and in these circumstances she could not enter the dry dock.

At 07:00 hours on the 24th she made an attempt, but on her first entry into the dry dock her bow paravane chains were hanging down and apparently knocked a few bilge blocks over. As the tide was about to change, the decision was made to pull her out of the dock again, pump the dock down and rebuild and reset the blocks. So the ship had to back out again and return to her anchorage in Royal Roads for twenty-four hours, all that time being a major target for U-boats, of which reports of sightings, off that part of the coast, were coming in throughout the night.

She eventually dry-docked the following morning with barely sufficient clearance on each side. On getting into the dock, there were a number of tugs to assist her. One small tug was very active, shoving in and doing her job. This was the US naval tug *Pawtucket*, whose zeal was somewhat subdued when she was suddenly caught between the towering sides of the *Queen Elizabeth* and some other larger tugs, which gave her quite a jolt. She did not actually capsize, but it must have seemed to those on board that she was in danger of so doing. She managed to manoeuvre out on to the edge of the crowded vessels and then took a less active role in the remaining docking operations!

Dry-docking enabled the *Elizabeth* to have a much-needed fumigation carried out. The crew were housed ashore in naval barracks and the officers booked into hotels. She was repainted with another protective colour, whilst two extra lifeboats, abaft the No 13 and 26 boats, were fitted in addition to the 3-in guns in the mounts on her foredeck, although no ammunition for these guns was available. Protective mountings for machine guns were fitted as well as plastic armour machine gun nests. Oerlikon ammunition lockers were provided and a telephone system was installed. It appeared, however, that in case of an air attack with all the guns in action the system would be inaudible so independent control would still be necessary. At the request of the Captain a 3-in Harvey Projector was relocated as it was considered to be dangerous to the crews of other guns. The kite was overhauled; two new paravanes installed (the former being lost!); the port Gallow's crane repaired; towing wires, inhauls, Blake Slips provided and repairs made to the port chain.

Special security was put around the dockyard while the *Queen Elizabeth* was there. The West Coast of Canada was very much at peace but the Royal Canadian Navy were given strict orders to let no one near the ship. They patrolled with old World War 1 rifles with bayonets and live ammunition and tried to persuade hundreds of sight-seers coming through the bush, to leave! Her hull was chipped and scraped of marine growth and after more than a week she left the dock to anchor in English Bay in Vancouver to take on oil and water.

At 10:00 hours on March 10 she sailed, escorted by a US destroyer until 09:30 the following day,

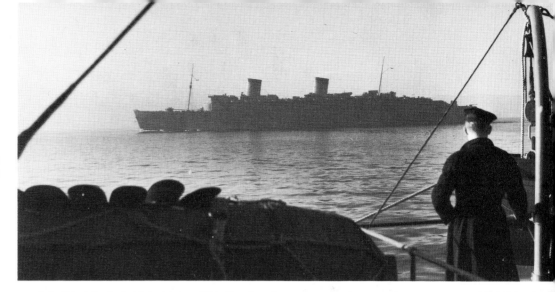

A sailor on an escorting vessel admires the view as she leaves Esquimalt (Public Archives, Canada).

A 'Golden-Gate' welcome! Queen Elizabeth *berths for her first and only visit to San Francisco, March 13 1942* (US National Archives).

Freshly painted, the Queen Elizabeth *is ready to leave 'Frisco Bay'* (US National Archives).

Above *USS* Salt Lake City *escorting a convoy in the Pacific Ocean, March 1942.*

Below *Convoy refuelling at Marquesas Island, March 1942. Drawing shows the transport* Mariposa.

to arrive in San Francisco on the morning of the 13th. Even a city as large as this was astounded to see such a ship moored at Pier 35. Immediately after she was berthed, the US Army Post Commander and his staff boarded. He was obviously impressed by the numbers the ship had ferried from Sydney to Suez but even so felt that the number could be increased even further—from 5,000 to 8,000. Within six days the ship was completely refitted by many working gangs who, by sawing and hammering, built many extra bunks, wherever possible, and even loose mattresses were used on the floor to help accommodate the extra passengers.

On March 19 she left San Francisco with some 8,000 American troops on board, in convoy with one heavy cruiser, the USS *Salt Lake City*, and two passenger ships *Mariposa* and *President Coolidge*. Many of the troops on board had never travelled beyond their own small towns before and quite a number were more than disturbed when they heard the bell ringing that accompanied the opening of the watertight doors. When the ship neared the coast or left harbour, all watertight doors were closed. To open them, one had to pull a lever and the door would open, making a noise and ringing a bell. The majority of the American troops were also ill informed about Australia and the area which they would eventually fight. Some of them evidently thought that Australia was a 'back-woods' country and that New Guinea was a holiday resort.

Refuelling again took place at Nuku Hiva and the natives there must indeed have been petrified when *Elizabeth* returned this time escorted by a cruiser and two other liners, and even more so when the *Coolidge* removed her excess steam, causing great white clouds to emerge and a lot of noise! This time the tanker had already arrived, so all four ships were immediately refuelled. There was some fear of Japanese carrier aircraft attacks at the anchorage and so troops were stationed at every promenade deck window with loaded rifles, ready to fire at any moment.

Following this refuelling the *Elizabeth* and her convoy set course for Sydney. Shortly before her arrival there two of the vessels were met by a New Zealand cruiser of the Achilles class, camouflage paintwork faded and rusted from long sea-keeping. This cruiser escorted the two American transports to a New Zealand port. The *Queen Elizabeth* proceeded, unescorted, to her port of call, arriving there on the afternoon of April 6. Just out of Sydney Heads, she passed the *Queen Mary*, which had just brought over her contingent of US Troops and was on her way back to New York.

On her arrival in Sydney shore labour was in such short supply that the ship's crew and some of the troops were engaged to off-load the baggage. Troops loaded it into cargo nets in the hold, while the crew acted as winchmen and hoisted up and lowered them into barges alongside. During these days some of these men received longshoremen's wages in addition to their own regular pay, for it was only on this condition that the union permitted this type of substitute labour to be carried out in Sydney. Some of this substitute labour worked from midnight until eight the following morning and had no sleep for three days. Sydney was absolutely crammed with shipping at the time!

After all had been disembarked and unloaded, the *Elizabeth* waited patiently to find out what would happen next for whilst on this trip further decisions had been made on her future role.

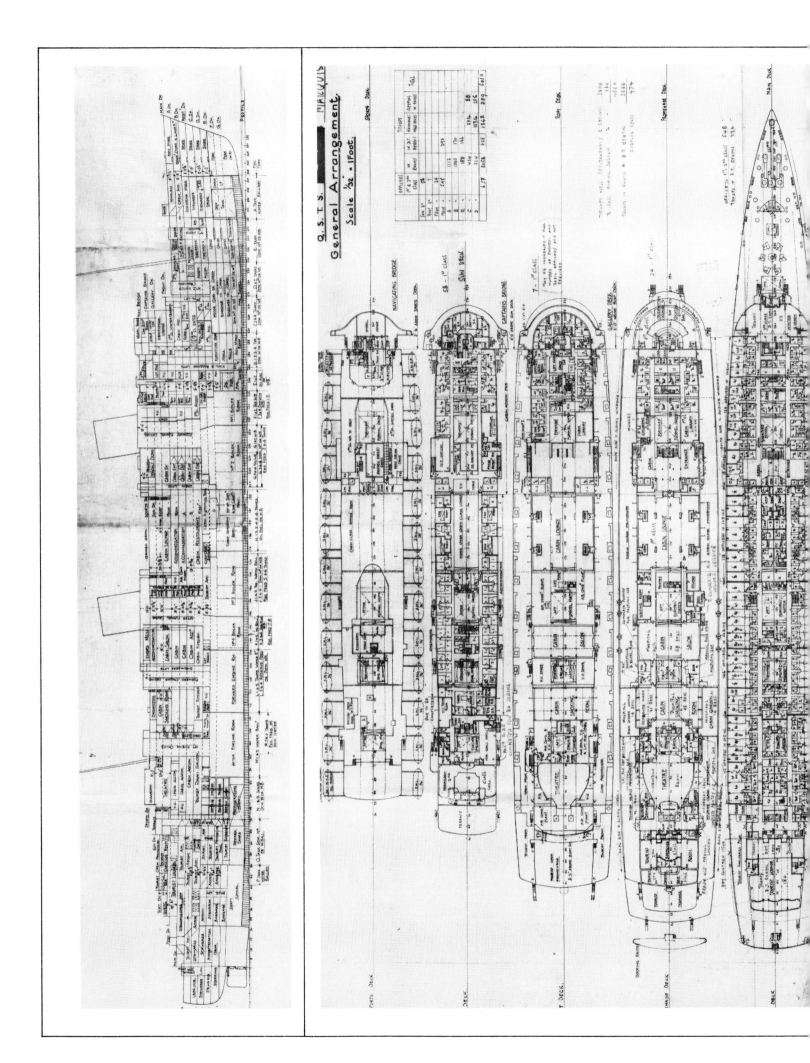

Q.S.T.S. MARQUIS.
General Arrangement. Scale 1/32 = 1Foot.

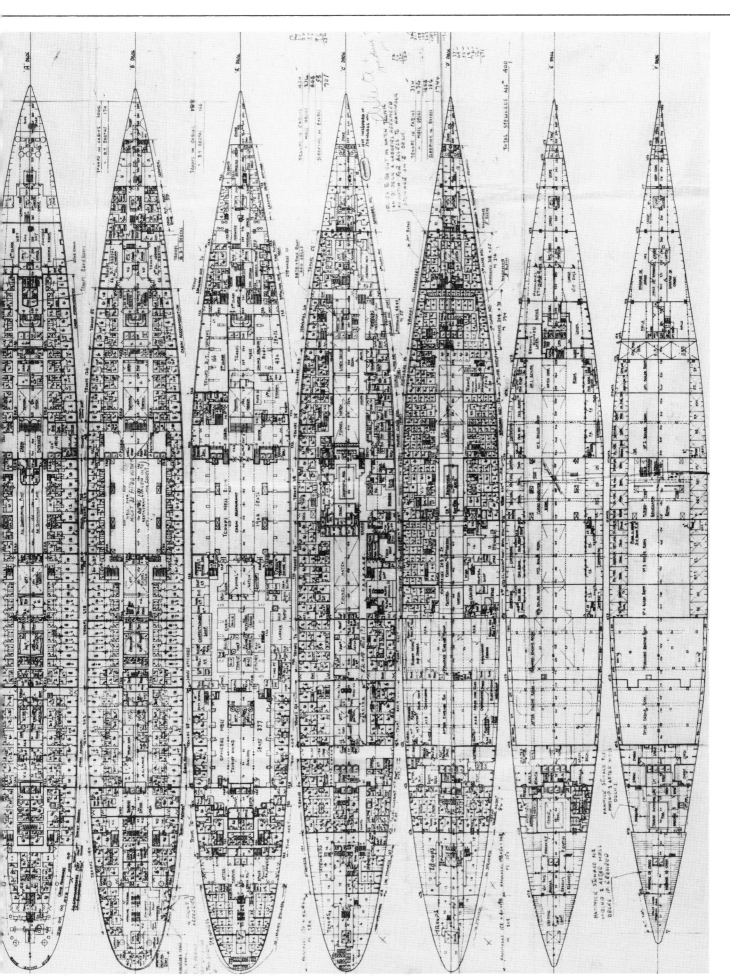

HMT Queen Elizabeth *general arrangement.*

Chapter 4

WS 19 Y

On March 25 1942, a letter from the War Office stated that the *Queen Elizabeth* would be placed at the British government's disposal for the movement of troops from the UK to the Middle East. As a result of negotiations between the British and the United States governments earlier that year, Prime Minister Churchill and President Roosevelt had discussed the possibility of shipping US troops to England. This would demonstrate to the world, and Germany in particular, that the Americans really wanted to finish the war as soon as possible, both in Europe and in the Far East, and that they wanted their troops to reach the front as quickly as possible. These American troops would complete their training in Europe and, thus allow the British to send reinforcements to the Middle East, where Rommel was trying to defeat them.

On the assumption that the *Queen Elizabeth* would be used to carry American troops to the UK and British troops to Suez, the following was the proposed programme:

Depart	New York	June 5
Arrive	UK	June 10
Depart	UK	June 17
Arrive	Freetown	June 25
Depart	Freetown	June 26
Arrive	Cape	July 2
Depart	Cape	July 3
Arrive	Suez	July 12

During this period the phases of the moon were new moon May 15 and June 13, and full moon April 30, May 30 and June 28, so the above programme fulfilled the following conditions: (a) She would not be in the UK or Suez during the full moon periods and: (b) She would not overlap a WS (Winston Special) convoy in the UK, Freetown, Cape Town or Suez. Therefore, it was proposed to have her sail from Sydney on or about April 18 1942, for New York via Cape Town and Rio de Janeiro. Australia seemed to be securely defended by now.

On Sunday, April 19, the *Queen Elizabeth* made her final departure from Australia, having been a familiar sight in Sydney Bay on many occasions during the past two years. On the top of Middle Head a lonely piper played a haunting lament on his bagpipes—Australia's farewell to a gallant Queen. In answer, the *Queen Elizabeth* blew three long blasts, which could be heard miles away—this was her final farewell to the hospitable people of Sydney.

On this trip the *Queen Elizabeth* took thirty nurses of the US 5th Station Hospital to Fremantle. As guests of the British they were treated royally, being the first women to travel on the ship. The ship's officers were kind enough to open the beauty salon for their use. It was the first time equipment such as the hairdryers had been used! For dining they were offered the use of the first class dining room and the food tasted so good that many of them gained up to 10 lbs on this short trip! The ship's main salon, furnished as for peacetime, was opened for their use and since there were a number of wounded Americans out of Corregidor on board, amongst whom there was a talented pianist, the nurses were entertained by the hour listening to him playing the grand piano. A very special item on this trip was an invitation to have tea with the Captain on the bridge during which they were also permitted to steer the great ship! British transports were 'wet' so the bar in the salon opened every day at 11.00 am. The night before they reached Fremantle they were treated to a champagne party.

A day or so before the ship reached Fremantle the ship suddenly turned around and headed due east at top speed to get away from an unidentified warship. That ship turned out to be the US cruiser *Phoenix* coming to escort her into port, but no one had told the Captain!

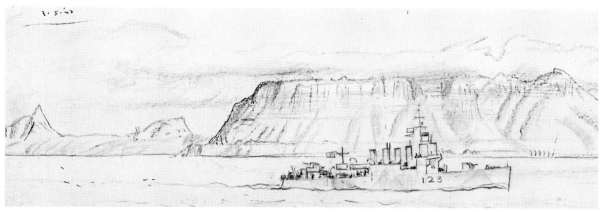

May 13 1942. A four-stacker escort in Table Bay.

After Fremantle to refill her oil and water tanks, it was off to Simonstown, South Africa, to pick up German POWs, who were to be transhipped from several other ships, one of them being the *Nieuw Amsterdam*, from which nearly 2,200 Germans were taken. Some 200 of them were officers, including two Generals. It was a cold day with a strong wind and a blue sky. The water was pretty choppy but the two ships, and it was often said that *Nieuw Amsterdam* was a smaller sister of the *Queen Elizabeth* in her appearance, made a beautiful sight.

Following this, the *Queen Elizabeth* headed for Rio de Janeiro to refuel, before going on to New York. Rio de Janeiro was a neutral port and refuelling was allowed if it could be undertaken within twenty-four hours. On May 16 at about 1000 hours, a strange freighter was sighted. Speed was increased to 30 kts and gun crews were at Action Stations but after a few hours the freighter was out of sight and speed was reduced again.

Nine days sailing from Rio brought the liner to New York again. First she anchored at the Quarantine Anchorage, in the Narrows, and when counting the heads it appeared that two POWs were missing. All shore-leave was cancelled and a great search for them started. They were eventually found in a locker, behind a bulkhead.

Many cars were travelling past on shore and crowds of people were waiting to see the *Queen Elizabeth* pass by, up the Hudson, before she berthed at Pier 90 again, having been away for about a year and a half. As time went on, big hoardings were put up to prevent passing traffic from seeing the ship.

Immediately she was alongside, the American Army transportation authorities came on board. The first thing they asked was how many people could be carried on board. Surprised when told 8,000, they caused even more surprise themselves when they said that they could increase the accommodation to carry an extra 2,000 before she sailed again—and this they did.

The ship was again overrun by hundreds of workmen because of the enormous amount of work to be carried out—painting, fitting of new bunks etc. It was planned that when the ship reached England a new degaussing housing would be fitted but meanwhile, the plating was put on board in New York. Preliminary work had already been carried out during her period in Esquimalt dry-dock. The degaussing cable, particularly where it went round the bow, at deck level, would sometimes come adrift in bad weather, so it was decided to plate it over right forward where it went inside the hull and where it would otherwise receive the full shock of a head sea in bad weather. The plates were stowed on the foredeck, along the forward coaming of the number one hatch, sheltered by the scuttle just ahead of the hatch.

Some crew members immediately got acquainted with New York Port Security. The centre of interest at that time was the *Normandie* (French Line), still lying on her side after a fire a few months previously. Some of the butchers on the *Queen*, shortly after their arrival in New York had a few hours off duty. They went down to their quarters and then noticed that there was a member of the FBI on board and two American soldiers with tommy-guns. The soldiers ordered the butchers to stand to attention and then asked them 'What came up through the port-hole?' The butchers had no idea what these men were talking about, but they were still ordered to open their lockers, which were searched thoroughly. Questions were asked by the soldiers and the G-man and the atmosphere was quite frightening.

It transpired that what actually triggered off this search was the fact that some Australians,

leaning out of the portholes, had asked some men in a nearby barge if they had any newspapers. When it was affirmed that they had, the Australians lowered down a rope. The men in the barge tied on the newspapers, which were then hauled back up and through the porthole. A patrolling watchman, very conscious of sabotage with the *Normandie* so close by, was immediately suspicious and reported the matter to the FBI: However, on further investigation the situation was soon remedied. Inasmuch as the *Queen*'s total stay in New York covered twelve days, the crew had ample time to sightsee and enjoy all the pleasures of a carefree New York, before departing for the UK on June 4.

Escorted by two cruisers, three Spitfires and two Liberator planes the *Queen Elizabeth* arrived at Gourock five days later, with her first load of American troops for Europe. The English crew had not been home for a long time so the Australians on board saw to it that their British colleagues had their four days of shore leave first. The remaining days were then divided between the Aussies, some of whom went to London or visited friends and relatives in various parts of Britain.

Well over 10,000 troops, part of the reinforcements for the Eighth Army, now came on board, the trip being the only voyage that was recorded as a Winston Special (WS 19Y). Rommel was heavily attacking the British Army in the desert and these troops were urgently needed there. It now became clear how great a part the *Queen Elizabeth* could play in the history of World War 2.

Because of her immense size and speed she could not only carry the equivalent number of troops to four other ships of 20,000 tons, but she was also able to reach her destination in half the time required by other convoys. It was her speed that became her greatest asset in carrying a very large number of troops.

Leaving the UK on June 17, she was escorted for a few hundred miles through the Bay of Biscay. On either bow she had three destroyers, at about half a mile distance, and another destroyer on either quarter, and right ahead an AA light cruiser. It was a pretty deadly place, the Bay of Biscay, in June 1942. A convoy was being attacked not far away on June 19, when a reconnaissance Focke-Wulf Kondor bomber made a sweep and approached from ahead, fairly low. Immediately the ship was at Action Stations and Fire Stations. The barrage from the cruiser ahead of the *Queen Elizabeth* gave the plane quite a surprise and he was happy to steer off and soon disappeared. A few hours after that the *Queen Elizabeth* encountered a dense fog, which made it impossible for the Germans to attack her.

Her limited endurance made it necessary to refuel somewhere on the voyage to Cape Town and Freetown seemed to be the only place, although it was hardly perfect for berthing. She arrived there late in the afternoon of June 25.

Freetown was called the 'White Man's Graveyard'. It was not really a suitable place for such a big ship. There was a very bad and difficult approach and there were strong currents with shallow water on the bar. The river was already congested with ships such as naval vessels and oil-tankers because Freetown was an important convoy staging port.

The entrance was swept and special buoys were laid for her to make it possible to go through the boom defence. At that time, all vessels were anchored in the river and refuelled by barges, which were taken out to the ships by tugs. Freetown was in possession of an oil jetty, but it was of limited strength and most certainly could not be used by the *Queen Elizabeth*. The area of activity was Government Wharf Jetty, which was a commercial port under the Sierra Leone Railways Department, where lighters were loaded or discharged.

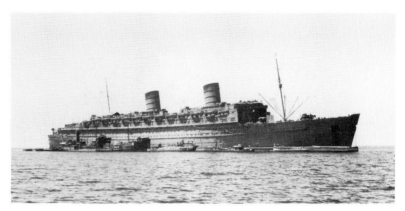

July 18 1942, Queen Elizabeth *anchored in the Red Sea with reinforcements for the 8th Army* (Imperial War Museum).

From Freetown, the *Elizabeth* went straight on to Cape Town and Simonstown where she arrived on July 2, leaving three days later for Suez, passing the *Queen Mary* and a convoy of six troop-ships, returning from the Red Sea, escorted by a Union Castle armed merchant cruiser (AMC).

Since there was no entertainment on board and with ever increasing temperatures, the crew organised a 'dance' in the sailor's messroom to give some zest to their life. It was arranged by the bosun's mate and some of the engineers, and all troops were welcome. Stewards, dressed in long dresses, would act as women and dance to the music of a gramophone, whilst liquid refreshment, in the form of beer, was being served. All tables were put aside and everyone had great fun. Soon, however, rumours started to spread to the effect that there were entertaining girls on the ship, and immediately the Officer Commanding, Troops, went down, escorted by several soldiers with guns and bayonets. 'These girls should be brought back' he said and was very annoyed. Inquiries started, sometimes in an unpleasant way. Arguments were not tolerated and if you did not co-operate you were made acquainted with the temperature of the .44 calibre rifle's steel!

A most interesting hearing was held the next morning. The Captain and the Staff Captain were extremely angry and upset at such a situation as (a) being dressed as girls was very much against the rules and could not be tolerated in a ship under strict discipline and (b) The OC Troops was not allowed to visit crew's quarters without permission. Punishment consisted of a strong reprimand and a reminder that the ship was in very dangerous waters where everyone should be very much aware of his task and of his duty to fight the enemy.

Imagine the thoughts of a German U-boat Kapitan, regarding British disipline, should he have seen these 'girls' floating around in the middle of the ocean, after torpedoing the ship? At that particular time, German submarines were refuelled and re-stored from Mozambique and the Strait of Mozambique had become a very dangerous spot. Later in 1942, the area became even more difficult when submarine mother-ships handled all this whilst at sea!

The *Queen Elizabeth* was like an oven and the Red Sea was intolerably hot. The British troops, not used to such intense heat, really suffered, as did the crew members, and many of the soldiers suffered from sunstroke. Temperatures in the cabins went up to 125° (F) and one can imagine the atmosphere those men lived in with all portholes closed. Working was also very hard. The crew in charge of preparing meals would sometimes go for a shower. They would walk under the shower, still dressed in shorts, singlets, boots and aprons, soak these thoroughly, and then return to their jobs again. Half an hour later they would be back to repeat this performance! Many of the troops slept on deck at night and hundreds of sea-water showers were improvised. Port Suez was reached on July 18 and the troops and medical personnel were disembarked, ready to take up their fight with the enemy in the desert.

As on previous occassions, several thousand POWs were embarked but, as the last ferry load was being prepared, an enemy plane was sighted. Shore batteries and ships opened up. It became too dangerous now to wait for the last load and the *Queen Elizabeth* sailed away with full speed on her engines. Within five hours she was well out of the danger area and on her way back to Cape Town.

The German prisoners were from Rommel's Afrika Korps and the majority of them were extremely arrogant and rude. However, with their sun-tanned faces and good looks they made a big impression on the crew. They were very fitness-conscious and did physical exercises every day for three hours from 05:00 to 08:00 hours. Most of them had been POWs for several months before

Left *Troops, disembarking at Port Tewfik, take a look back at the liner* (Imperial War Museum).

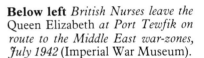

Below left *British Nurses leave the* Queen Elizabeth *at Port Tewfik on route to the Middle East war-zones, July 1942* (Imperial War Museum).

being put on this transport. The prisoners were not allowed to eat with knives and forks, because these could be collected and used as weapons. Nor were they allowed to use pepper as this could be saved up and thrown in the eyes of the guards.

This time their guards were Poles, some of whom were very young, just boys from sixteen years of age, who were armed mainly with small Italian rifles. They all stood their share of duties and were not afraid of anyone. They had had a bad time before joining the ship but the Germans had respect for them—they knew that these guards would shoot first and ask questions later! A favourite trick of some of the POWs was to try to expose light at night, hoping that the ship would be sunk by a German raider or submarine. Some tried to escape, as happened when the ship was in Simonstown again. At first she had to proceed to Cape Town, but on arrival there the swell was too big to get a tanker alongside to refuel. Orders were then changed to proceed to Simonstown on the morning of August 3 1942. At that time some Germans jumped overboard, which was rather foolish, for the ship was well off the coast, the weather was bad, the water was cold and it was very difficult to swim wearing a uniform. Immediately a ship's boat was lowered to pick them up. Unfortunately, one of the Germans was killed on being struck by the boat and the others drowned. To this present day, though, it is still rumoured that one of them reached the coast safely! After this unhappy incident, the *Queen Elizabeth* was refuelled and set course for Rio de Janeiro.

En route to Rio the weather was perfect and the ship carried out a series of speed trials. Cooks and stewards had stacked piles of plates on the hot presses for the morning meals before taking a break, when the quartermaster steering the ship had to go to the toilet. (The water which had been taken on at Simonstown was foul and most of the crew were toilet prone.) The quartermaster was unable to find his relieving colleague, so in desperation he instructed a bridge man to take over for a few minutes. This particular man had steered the ship before and so he was instructed to use very little helm, if any, as she was taking very little at these trials. As usual, when steering well, you have a steady tick-tick on the gyro-repeater, but apparently this man tried to stop the tick and put a lot of helm on, causing the ship to heel over badly. This caused all the breakfast plates in the galley to slide and break! Fortunately, the quartermaster brought her back as slowly as possible, to avoid more damage.

Above *Crew members 'Red' Hunt, Syd Middleton 'Unknown' and Paul Cramer relaxing on the foredeck at Port Tewfik, 1942. Note young Polish Guard, age 14, in centre of picture.*

Below *HMS* Valiant *off Simonstown Navy Base.*

A British cargo vessel off Simonstown.

In order to avoid escapes from the ship at Rio de Janeiro, an order was given that no one must put his head out of the porthole. Two motor launches with armed guards were patrolling all night, assisted by the search lights, which slashed the water in irregular patterns.

The ship's doctor, Dr Maguire, was very pleased to be back in Rio again. It gave him the opportunity to keep the portholes open for a while, there being no need for a blackout, as Rio was a neutral port. In this way the ship would get some extra fresh air. One of the medical orderlies thought he would acquire a little more of this refreshing commodity by keeping his head close to the porthole. Not content with this, however, he stuck his head a little way out, but had the shock of his life when some rounds of machine gun were let off and bullets started flying around his head.

In Rio, the German Consul came round in his launch with the Swastika flag flying and taking many different photographs. This caused some excitement amongst the Germans on board, who knew this place would have been a perfect spot for escaping!

Of course there was always a chance of a submarine attack when leaving the three-mile zone of neutral waters, but by then her speed was already so great that it was impossible for the submarines to estimate in which direction she was travelling and so the *Queeen Elizabeth* safely crossed the ocean again to reach Ambrose Lightship on August 19.

The Germans were ferried ashore again at the Quarantine Base by the Canadian Provost Corps, to be sent to Canada by train. The ferry came to a shell door in the ship's hull and the Afrika Korps were searched by the Canadians for any papers and weapons which they might have concealed on their person. The search yielded all kinds of makeshift weapons, some being made from spoons, for example, which were sharpened on the edges and used as 'epaulettes'. Razor blades were stuck in the wooden panelling and even Australian soldiers' paybooks were found. The watch on the shell door was struck by the rough way in which the Canadians handled the Germans, since the Germans were not defiant or showing any fight. Not that they struck them, just that the pushing and shoving was uncalled for, particularly as the Canadians were all 'giants and pretty tough hombres'.

The crew was very tired after this boring and uneventful voyage to tropical waters and on top of this New York was also like a furnace. Many of them decided to leave the vessel and were determined not to return to Suez again. Interestingly, they might not have had any choice as at this time the ship was very close to being converted into an aircraft carrier.

Chapter 5

Aircraft carrier conversion?

In April 1942 it was thought that Britain should get as many aircraft sea-borne as possible. One way of doing so was to convert the largest liners or some of them, into aircraft carriers. Owing to their large size, turning circle, etc, they would obviously be unsuitable for working with the Royal Navy, but they would be able to carry a large number of bomber planes and possibly these planes could land in some territory belonging to Britain, having made their attacks.

Investigation into the feasibility of this concept was initiated and the following were considered as possible functions for such a ship: (a) bomb Japan, aircraft to land in China; (b) bomb Singapore, aircraft to land in Australia; (c) reinforce areas with large numbers of fighters or light bombers; and (d) support of combined operations.

The conversion would not take more than 12-15 months and it was felt that the Americans would be very enthusiastic to undertake such work, far more so than the British. There were only three firms in the UK who could carry out that work, namely; John Brown & Co, Harland & Wolff and Cammell Laird.

Investigations were confined to the *Queen Elizabeth* and a short-term policy was also considered, ie, to build a flight deck, leaving the funnel uptakes in place.

The beam of the *Queen Elizabeth* would enable large aircraft to be erected aft and wheeled forward of the funnels for take off; however to form the after end of the ship into a flight deck, for landing on, would not be a practical proposition, owing to wind disturbance over the deck caused by the funnel uptakes. It was not possible to give a forecast of the number of aircraft that could be carried or what size of aircraft was envisaged. These factors all depended on what kind of lifts would be fitted. American lifts were 45 ft long by 45 ft wide and had the advantage that a greater number of fighters could be got into the

air more quickly as three folding aircraft could be brought up together.

The main particulars of the *Queen Elizabeth* as an aircraft carrier would have been as follows:

Length overall 1,025 ft (approx)
Beam 118 ft
Max width of flight deck 143 ft 6 ins
Draught 38 ft (approx)
Speed 29 kts normally, with a possible max of 31½ kts. (It was estimated that converting her into an aircraft carrier could add 3 kts to her normal speed)
Displacement 72,000 tons
Armament four twin 4-in guns, five 8-barrelled pom-poms
Aircraft 60 folded bombers/fighters 40 ft × 18 ft or 84 folded bombers/fighters 44 ft × 13 ft 6 ins (minimum width in way of island)
Endurance Approx 9,000 miles at 25 kts
Petrol 120,000 gallons
'Flying-on' deck 460 ft × 125 ft
'Flying-off' deck (port side) 500 ft × 63 ft 6 ins
'Flying-off' deck (starboard side) 47 ft 6 ins (minimum width in way of island)
Accelerators two—one port and one starboard
Aircraft lifts two—each 45 ft × 34 ft (possibility of a third lift was being investigated)
Hangars two—each 672 ft × 45 ft × 16 ft minimum clear height
Arresting wires 6
Safety barriers 2

Space was available for torpedo stowage, bombs, ammunition and aircraft maintenance on the usual scales.

John Brown's estimated that the time of conversion would be from nine to twelve months but, as the work would probably be undertaken in the United States, it would be safer to assume twelve to fifteen months. They were requested to investigate this re-design, as they had the

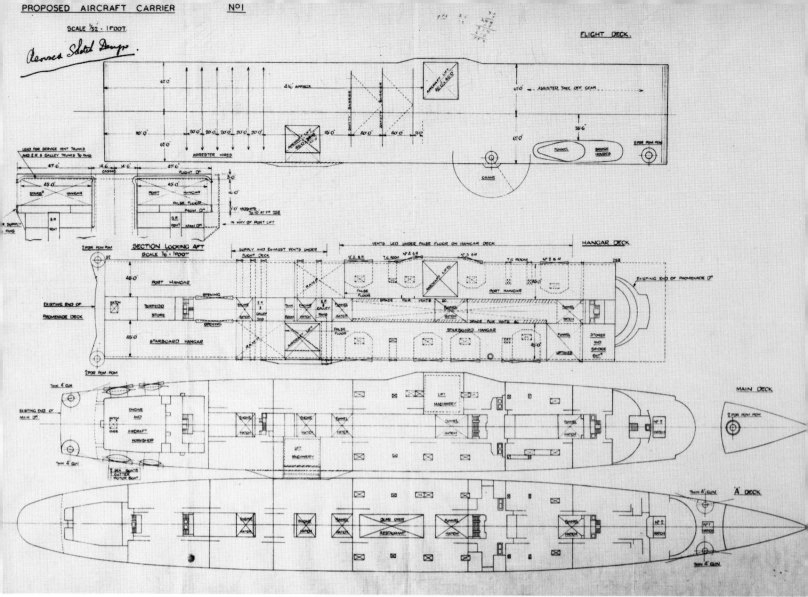

Proposed aircraft carrier conversion.

necessary staff available for this work and, of course, had the knowledge of the details of the design of this ship.

Accordingly, arrangements were made for a representative of the Ministry of Defence to visit John Brown & Co and the firm was requested to make a model on the assumption that the airflow experiments would be undertaken at the National Physics Laboratory. John Brown's wanted to make a model of the simplest possible type as it was considered that a quick series of experiments, which would give approximate tendencies, was indicated, rather than an elaborate and accurate set of trials.

The question of what type of lifts were to be used caused some discussion. The size and number of lifts and also the possibility of fitting an island arrangement to take a funnel on the starboard side forward, were also discussed with John Brown's, resulting in the following proposals:

(a) *Island structure:* The bridge and funnel could be placed on the starboard side forward in accordance with normal aircraft-carrier practice. This involved considerable dislocation of the systems existing in the ship, but it was John Brown's opinion that this extra work could be carried out concurrently with the work of reconstruction and that, if properly organised, it should not extend the date of completion for the whole job.

(b) *Number of lifts:* John Brown's stated that they would strongly favour the two-lift arrangement for reasons of top weight and strength compensations. They also assumed that if the third lift were to be placed at the after end, it would cause considerable disturbance of the boat stowage and the after deck-house.

(c) *Size of lifts:* John Brown's produced a scheme whereby the two lifts could each be 45 ft × 45 ft, but of course it was still recommended that they should be 45 ft × 35 ft, unless the larger lifts met definite requirements which could not be met by the smaller ones. Experience showed that it would be essential to have more room for the structural strength of the flight deck on the outboard side of the lift than was possible in John Brown's arrangement. With the bridge and funnel brought out on the starboard side to form an island, a certain amount of hangar space was lost and the number of aircraft that could be stowed became less.

If the conversion was approved and assuming that arrangements were made for the work to be undertaken in the USA, it was suggested that a number of John Brown's draughtsmen, aquainted with the ship, should go to America to give technical assistance.

At the end of all these discussions, John Brown's considered that, if all necessary preparatory work was done before the ship was taken in hand for conversion and if items such as lift machinery, arresting gear and other large items were prepared beforehand the actual conversion work would not take more than six to seven months. The revised design for the *Queen Elizabeth* made a flight deck of 730 ft or only about 10 ft less than that of the *Illustrious* class carriers.

This design was revised due to the fact that the size of the ship gave the false impression that large aircraft could be easily embarked. In actual fact, the hangar dimensions of 16 ft height, by 45 ft width, did not allow for any aircraft larger than naval types or fighters. It was considered that the loss of capacity was outweighed by the advantage of a clear flight deck, especially as the work involved would not delay the ship coming into carrier service.

Meanwhile, other attributes of the *Queen Elizabeth* played their part as well. For instance, the size of the ship could not be ignored. When berthed at anchor she required 3¼ cables swinging room from the nearest land and there were only a few ports available to dock her as an aircraft carrier. The question of her turning circles at 15 and 25 knots was raised as well. No turning trials had ever been carried out, but the Marine Superintendent thought that the manoeuvring capabilities of the *Queen Elizabeth* would compare favourably with the largest type of naval ship. It was estimated that the time needed for turning equalled at least that necessary to go 2½ times the length of the ship, according to the speed.

Another factor discussed was her flexibility in speed—could she increase or decrease it rapidly? The *Queen Elizabeth* was visited by an officer of the Ministry of Defence on June 13 1942. Acceleration rates were discussed with Sir Stephen Pigott of John Brown's, Mr Austin, Marine Superintendent of the Cunard Company, and the ship's Engineer Officer.

Subject to adequate training of personnel and possibly to additional telegraphs, the following rates could readily be obtainable without risk of damage to machinery: from 15 kts to 25 kts, 20 minutes; and from 15 kts to 28 kts, 35 minutes. Possibly this time might be further reduced, but these figures already were something of a reduction from the previously accepted time, which was one and a half hours. With regard to decreases in speed, the ship could come to a stop from 27½ knts in ten minutes.

Then there was also the matter of how great her fuel consumption really was. The original 9,000 miles estimated range, was based on trial results but, since then, they had revised their estimates making allowance for weather and the additional wind resistance of the superstructure, to give a new figure of 6,000 miles.

Considering all this, it was finally concluded that the ship could be used as (a) an unarmoured fleet carrier and (b) an aircraft transport. If employed as a fleet carrier, she would have handled reasonably well, but her great size would have made her an attractive target. Her endurance would have been ample but the difficulties of docking in case of damage made it preferable that she operate within three thousand miles of the North American coast or Great Britain since the only available dry docks were now very limited.

This limitation, the time it would have required to convert her and a rather weak armament were the principal objections, and in view of the important part she was playing in the movement of troops it was considered that she would be best retained in her present employment.

By this time the Allied forces were advanced in their plans for liberating Europe. For that purpose one million men needed to be moved from the USA to the UK by April 1943, and negotiations to use the *Queen Elizabeth* for this purpose had begun!

Four alternative schemes were put forward: (i) ferrying across the Atlantic on three weeks' turnaround, with the risk of the programme becoming known to the enemy; (ii) sailings from New York to Cape Town or to Suez, fed by returning westbound transports; (iii) as (ii) but sailing from the Clyde; and (iv) Pacific sailings from the USA, as before, if the USA would like the ship used for this service.

The question was whether scheme (i) could be acceptable, or if another programme was to be preferred. The Director of Plans was not keen to have her employed on a transatlantic service because there was a risk of her programme

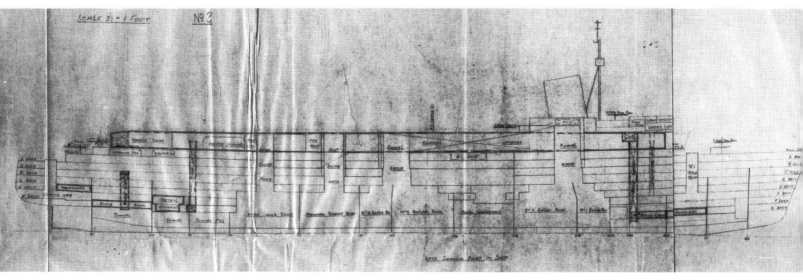

Proposed aircraft carrier conversion, profile.

becoming known to the enemy and the ship being ambushed, bombed or torpedoed. The lack of facilities for the ship at Greenock and consequent waste of time in turning her round between a series of comparatively short voyages was also a consideration.

Of the alternatives, the Director of Plans preferred to have her sail to Suez again, as given in scheme (iii), but in one of his letters he also stated. 'If, however, in order to implement the movement of this large number of Americans to the UK in the time required, the *Queen* is necessary on the Atlantic Run, I think we should accept the risk to the ship, provided the Americans will accept the risk to the troops.'

A lively discussion started betweeen those who were pro or contra the Director's ideas. Those who were against his ideas believed that if it was decided the ship was necessary to carry the proposed number of troops over the Atlantic, or that a ferry service should be inaugurated, it should have a four-weekly turnaround to fit in with the lunar periods. Also they stated that the current schedule by which she, first, brought US troops to the UK, second, sailed with British troops from the Clyde to Suez and, third, proceeded empty to New York, was much to be preferred (this arrangement was known as the 'Triangular Schedule'). In this way the amount of time spent in the dangerous submarine areas both on the east and west sides of the Atlantic was reduced to a minimum. They proposed, too, that the programme should be adjustable so that by holding the ship at New York on each occasion as

necessary, her trips could fit the phases of the moon and programmes of other convoys.

Not everyone agreed with these points. Some were in favour of the ship starting the Atlantic ferry service. These felt that the *Queen Elizabeth* should be used in the most economical way and her safety on the Atlantic was being emphasised over-anxiously. She was built for this service, so presumably she was best suited for this passage. High speed, the darkness at sea, fighter planes and AA-gun defence in harbours, would give adequate security. Apart from which, her crew would hardly be able to touch England if she sailed on the Triangular Schedule.

The Director of Movements was very anxious to give Washington some estimate of the British-controlled shipping that would be made available during 1942 for the movements of American forces to the UK and asked the War Office for a speedy decision. This he received next day when, in a message to the British Army Staff in Washington, it was mentioned that the Admiralty was prepared to accept the *Queen Elizabeth* continously on the Atlantic passage as her speed was considered to give reasonable security against submarines whilst an adequate degree of AA defence could be provided within aircraft range of the UK and in the Clyde. In that way she would also avoid more serious risks in the Indian Ocean and at Suez.

The British would operate the liner and pay the crew, whilst the Americans would organise her as best suited US interests, providing food and bedding for the troops.

Chapter 6

Atlantic voyages—the mechanics of crossing

Now the most important, but also the most monotonous, period of the *Queen Elizabeth*'s war service began. In nearly three and a half years she would make over thirty Atlantic crossings, starting from New York or Halifax, ferrying US and Canadian troops to Europe.

One of the first questions asked was how many troops could be carried on one voyage. Sir Winston Churchill wrote in his memoirs about the discussion he had on this matter with General George Marshall.

General Marshall had observed the *Queen* and noticed that boats, rafts and other life-saving gear could only be provided for approximately 8,000 troops. On the other hand, if one could disregard all this, it was easily possible for the ships to carry about 16,000 men. On a trip which lasted only a few days, a larger number of passengers could obviously be accommodated than when she was crossing the Pacific or Indian Ocean; supplying the ship with more rafts was considered to be practicable as well.

Churchill could only tell him what Britain would do in a case like this and General Marshall had to judge for himself, as to the risks he thought he could take. Thus the Prime Minister wrote that if it was the plan to move a vast amount of troops in the quickest way possible across the Atlantic, as part of an operation, Churchill would have put on board as many as the ship could carry. If, however, it was simply a question of moving them there in a reasonable time, Churchill would not carry more than 10,000 men in order not to go beyond the limits of the life-saving gear. The decision was made. Marshall accepted the risks and thought of the previous voyages the ship had run. In the last two years she had carried many thousands of troops and fortune had always been on her side, so why not for this operation as well?

First, though, extensive refits had to be made in the ship's interior, for the intention now was to pack her as closely as possible with troops. For this purpose, the hammocks and wooden bunks with which the Australians had equipped the liner, were removed and were then replaced by that ingenious invention, the 'Standee bunk'.

This was a stretcher-like construction, supported on tubular steel uprights and made of canvas, slung on poles. These only took up a small amount of space, which was their main advantage. The cocktail bar, the swimming pools and the cabins were all gradually filled with these bunks, leaving a few rooms and lounges to be used as dining rooms, troops offices or for any VIPs making the crossing. Every available space was utilised—many staterooms now accommodated ten or twelve times the number of passengers they were intended for in peacetime. During the daytime, when all the rooms needed cleaning, one could easily hinge these bunks upwards and secure them with a chain and hook. In fact, the only parts of the *Queen Elizabeth* that were left clear were the alley-ways and companion-ways.

After a few months ferrying, plying across the Atlantic, the question was raised as to whether it was sensible to carry around 15,000 troops during the winter months. The *Queen Elizabeth* had the habit of rolling slowly but very heavily, a problem which also occurred with her sister ship. This was noticed by Sir James Bisset, when he observed the *Queen Mary*'s zig-zagging and her roll due to helm movement. In addition to this, he saw that she also had a jerky movement, likely to be accentuated by the large number of troops. This went on to such an extent that Sir James was concerned about the stability of his ship. He had not noticed such movement when carrying only 11,000 troops. He considered 'that such a large number on board during the winter months, when the Atlantic is at its worst, would cause the ordinary heavy rolling to be accentuated as the men would "go" with the ship's roll. It was not possible to get men to lie down for several days and, unlike cargo which would remain stable, they would "move" with the ship, which in rough weather had a roll of up to 25 degrees.' He also pointed out that the Standee bunks were rather unsuitable for the Atlantic winter voyages, as the men would fall out of them when the ship rolled heavily. Commodore Irving, of the *Queen Elizabeth*, thought that many men would therefore get broken limbs, which would necessarily put a strain on the ship's medical staff.

But there was another point which drew the Master's close attention. Her armament and adjacent ammunition lockers added considerable top weight to the ship, which reduced her stability. In fact, it raised her centre of gravity (G) about 300 mm. There were about 150 tons of wire in the degaussing coils about 42 ft above the waterline. This raised her G 210 mm. The total daily consumption of fuel plus water was about 1,700 tons; which would cause G to rise another 240 mm per day, so at the end of a five-to six-day voyage, a total rise of approximately 1,250 mm would be accumulated.

Background photograph *Bunkering from a Canadian coastal tanker,* HMT Queen Elizabeth *prepares to leave Halifax, Nova Scotia* (Public Archives, Canada).
Inset photograph *Troops relaxing below decks in crowded quarters* (University Archives, University of Liverpool).

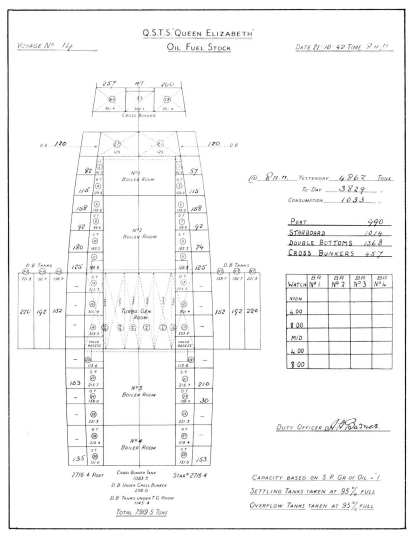

Then there was boat drill which, assuming 15,000 troops to weigh about 1,100 tons, meant that this weight would move upwards to the boat deck for about 15 meters, causing G to rise 200 mm as well. Towards the end of a voyage, G was quite high and the ship required careful handling, especially when boat drill was being held.

There was also the possibility that the ship would heel over dangerously if the rudder was put hard over in an emergency (the normal practice was not to use more than 5° rudder on altering course). To compensate for this heel, salt water could be pumped into the fresh-water and oil tanks for ballasting. This was undesirable due to consequent contamination of the tanks and pollution of the sea if the tanks were pumped out again. The oily water would have to pass through a separator or be pumped into special lighters or tanks in port. In the case of the fresh-water tanks, a lot of fresh water would have to be pumped through the tanks to make sure that they had been sweetened. However, in case of a serious attack by planes or enemy ships, these methods would certainly be used.

Stability of the ship was calculated every day using the fuel and fresh water reports, and it was on account of fears for her stability that she was not sent into ice-fields whenever possible. At last, after further discussions, it was decided that in the winter months her capacity would not exceed 12,000 men and that only the lower Standee

Left Queen Elizabeth *Engineer's daily oil report.*
Below *Leaving America for Gourock, Scotland, crammed with US troops. Note the vessel's heavy extra armament (US National Archives).*

bunks would be used. In the summer period, which existed from May until September, her average load never fell below 15,000 men.

However, in winter, even with only the smaller number of troops, dangerous situations could arise. In February 1944 the *Queen Elizabeth* was encountering a heavy storm when nearing the coast of Northern Ireland. The ship was rolling very heavily and the quartermaster on watch found it almost impossible to keep her on course. The more he tried, the more she rolled. Suddenly the ship took a frightening list to port. In the wheelhouse people could see the sky on one side and the sea on the other! The quartermaster had her wheel 'hard a' starboard' and told the Captain that she didn't answer her helm. She now took an even bigger list to port, and the Captain gave the order to 'let her go'. The wheel came back midships and slowly she started to right herself again. Meanwhile she had drifted some 90 degrees off course and the inclinometer showed her greatest list as 37 degrees. A few more degrees could have had her capsized.

The Americans had pointed out that 8,000 Standees was the perfect number, for no man sleeps 24 hours in a day. Half the number of troops would use the bunk to sleep, whilst the other half would be engaged elsewhere. In some cases, the bunks were used by three men and because of this it was decided to have extra Standees installed on the promenade deck. This would increase the sleeping accommodation and also enable a larger number of troops to be carried. Because these bunks were unheated, they

were not used in the winter period and during this time many troops slept in the alley-ways.

One major problem confronting the authorities was the provision of sufficient numbers of life-saving devices which, in the case of an emergency, would give everyone on board a reasonable chance of survival. The *Queen Elizabeth* carried a life-boat certificate for 4,000 persons—certainly inadequate in view of the fact that she was carrying four times that number. An extra pair of life-boats was installed aft of the number 13 and 26 life-boats in Esquimalt, and the ship carried sufficient rafts now to float free. However, if the vessel had been hit in bad weather, the loss of life would have been appalling as indeed it would have been under any circumstances—rafts or no rafts!

Frequently many of these rafts were washed over the side. Of course, everyone had a life-jacket—the famous 'Mae West'—which was to be worn on drill and carried around throughout the voyage. Anyone seen without one had to surrender his shoes immediately and no exceptions were made. It was a very simple method of impressing upon those on board the desirability of never leaving your life-jacket!

Life-boat drills were held frequently and were aimed at moving troops as quickly as possible to the boat stations. On the alarm bells sounding, the troops would work their way upwards to the boat deck and promenade deck. On the first two days of the crossing there were two drills a day and then one daily. On the first drill it would take the men about half an hour to reach the stations and many would not have reached their goal

Below *Photographed from an escorting aircraft at 400 ft altitude* (US National Archives).

before the stairways were hopelessly jammed. After four or five drills the time taken to jam everyone onto the top decks would be about ten minutes!

Prominent, painted arrows, indicating direction, displayed in conjunction with the words 'Emergency Stations', were the only really satisfactory feature of the tallying within the ship. In all other respects, tallying was thoroughly inadequate. Thousands of service personnel and a considerable number of civilians were embarked in a matter of hours, the majority of them complete strangers to seafaring. Many of them became hopelessly lost and often it took them hours to find their accommodation. Very few, within 24 hours of embarking, had knowledge of alternative routes from point to point on any one deck, nor did they, within that same period, make use of any other but the main stairway. On no account were lifts to be used by troops or their officers.

As an illustration of the type of disorder that occurred, on one occasion during embarkation at New York, the unit commanders completely lost touch with their units and groups of men lost touch with the main body of their units. After eighteen hours of absolute chaos, the men accommodated on the promenade deck overnight were ordered to exchange places with an equal number accommodated below—the so-called box and cox change-over routine. Those above, overburdened with kit, attempted to struggle down the stairways up which others were mounting. To make matters worse the emergency signal was given while the change-over was in hand. (The American staff had failed to notify the Staff Captain.) Surprisingly there was no panic,

Sign-board on the main stairway, explaining the various signals which may be given on board whilst at sea (Imperial War Museum).

but at least two hours elapsed before order could be completely restored.

On another occasion, even 48 hours after leaving New York, some troops had not found their accommodation. Some found their way to the Naval Regulating Office (forward) only to learn that they should retrace their steps to the main stairway, thence . . . etc! On a number of occasions, due to increasing U-boat activity in the Atlantic, the ship suddenly had to alter course. This would cause the ship to heel over and the handling of the ship then became very difficult, especially when Emergency Stations was sounded, or life boat drill was in hand.

The following observations, to illustrate the need for remedial action, were submitted:

'Existing tallying:
1. Deck-name plates—too few and, when stairways are crowded, these are inconspicuous.
2. Cabin numbers—characters are crudely painted; many are only half an inch in depth.
Suggestions:
1. Additional and conspicuous deck-name plates.
2. Cabin numbers—characters of at least two inches and their appropriate block should be stencilled.
3. In main alley-ways—
(a) "STARBOARD", "PORT", "FORWARD", "AFT".
(b) "CABIN NOS . . . TO . . . "
(c) " . . . SECTION", "CANTEEN", "HOSPITAL", etc.
  In cross passages—(a) "cabin nos . . . to . . . "
    (b) " . . . Section"
Note To indicate ALTERNATIVE route from one section to adjacent section, when at sea, intervening door is "CLOSED". ARROWS should be displayed in conjunction with the above and "sections" to be re-named throughout, and ship's drawings brought up to date.'

To get some order, the ship was divided vertically into three zones, each of which had its own distinctive colour: *red* was forward, from bow to the main entrance, with a Royal Navy Commander in charge; *white* was midships, from main entrance aft to the entrance abaft the officers' dining room on R deck, with a Canadian Army Lieutenant in charge; and *blue* was from the entrance on R deck, abaft of the officers' dining room aft to the stern, with a Royal Air Force Wing-Commander in charge. Each section had an orderly room now serving as the regimental headquarters, and contact between the sections was maintained by telephone or runner; these communications were excellent and used extensively. All headquarters operated 24 hours a day and divisional commanders could contact their subordinate units with a minimum of delay.

Upon embarking on the ship, each man was given a coloured tag, corresponding to the area he had been assigned to and designating the area of the ship he could use. The men had to wear these tags at all times and Military Police checked for this continuously. It also showed the number and time of their mess-sitting and when going to the messroom at mealtimes, the only time they could go from one area to another, again MPs kept the traffic moving in an orderly fashion. In the narrow alley-ways a one-way traffic system was

necessary, which was operated on an anti-clockwise basis; forward on the starboard side and aft on the port side.

Once all were on board, the ship could sail. The most important of the safety devices was now to play her part. For at least five days she would sail without any escort, depending instead on her high speed, but unable to predict if there was an enemy submarine or ship waiting half-way across the ocean. The organisers behind all the planning of her voyages, made a tremendous effort to avert all dangers and to have the troops arrive safely at their destination. Thus British Admiralty and the American Navy pointed out precisely the route

A selection of cards issued to troops and ship's personnel.

the *Queen Elizabeth* had to follow, and the time she was due to arrive at her destination. The phases of the moon were still taken into account.

A report of August 1942 noted that earlier it had been approved for her to operate on the North Atlantic, provided she would be in England during the dark period. This resulted in making one round voyage per lunar month, for 11 days of which she would be idle in New York.

This, of course, could be improved upon and it was thought that by accepting only slight additional risks, she could be in England at any time during the month other than four days either side of a full moon.

Allowing five days for the passage in each direction, three days turn-around in the Clyde and five days turn-around in New York, the ship could make the round voyage in a minimum of 18 days and in that way more troops could be carried. The discussion as to whether the 28-days schedule was the most practicable or not, went on into late 1943. It meant that 46,000 troops less could be carried in half a year: some of these figures would be compensated for in the winter, when a more rigid schedule could be handled, there being longer dark hours. At last the decision was made that the *Queen Elizabeth* had to sail as quickly as possible, for troops were urgently needed, enemy submarines or not!

Because of the constant threat that the enemy might get hold of the ship's sailing schedule and routes, their communication to the ship's Captain and navigation officer was very carefully planned. Approximately two hours before she left port, the Captain, accompanied by his Chief Navigating Officer, his Radio Officer and Cipher Officer went ashore. In the Naval Control Office they were given the route, detailed as precisely as

possible. The route showed courses, speed, zig-zags and all the latest information on the whereabouts of U-boat concentrations, icebergs and the positions of convoys or of any other ship which could be near her route. They were also informed as to where and when they could rendezvous with an air or surface escort.

Then the latest signal-code books were handed over, as well as maps and instructions on how to break radio silence, in the event that this should prove necessary. Routes were very often changed and information on such changes would be relayed to them by radio. By the same means they were sometimes advised to avoid a new convoy or U-boat, and also the names of ships, whose codes had been broken and whose position had become known, were passed on to them. It was very unusual for the route not to be changed during the voyage.

Occasionally she was routed well north, on one such occasion she was in the latitude of 60° and passed quite close to Cape Farewell, Greenland, although the cape itself was not sighted. Icebergs were a constant danger on the western side, especially in spring. Once, in July 1943, on the westbound voyage, just a day or two prior to arrival in New York, an iceberg was seen. However, it was alone and was subsequently used for target practice!

Fastening the ship's gear didn't change from peacetime routine. Prior to leaving the pier or anchorage the ship was made ready for sea and was 'squared up'. Hatches were battened, cargo booms lowered, clamped and stripped of their gear; wire runners and boom guys were coiled up and passed through a deck man-hole for stowing in lockers on A deck below. When departing from a pier the mooring lines were passed below and

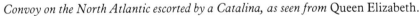

Convoy on the North Atlantic escorted by a Catalina, as seen from Queen Elizabeth.

coiled down on A deck. Quite often the rope falls of the boom topping lifts were 'frapped' to the shrouds of the lower rigging once the vessel was under way. Usually the lookout's task, it was a freezing job working aloft bare-headed, heading down NY harbour in the dead of winter.

Once at sea, the *Queen Elizabeth* started her zig-zag pattern, which she had to follow all the way through and which was listed in a 'ZZ' book, distributed by the Royal Navy. The ship frequently used ZZ no 8, which had a distance loss of 7 per cent. It was a relatively simple pattern and involved course alterations of 25° and 50°, and was repeated every 40 minutes.

On the bridge a ZZ clock was installed, together with a blackboard. This was an ordinary clock, but modified to buzz at chosen times. The minute hand had a metal 'whisker' attached to its tip. A collar fitted to the clock could have metal contacts screwed on at any part of its circumference. When the whisker met the contact a buzzer, powered by dry-cell batteries, sounded. The blackboard near the helmsman listed times, course, alterations and next course to be steered. On hearing the buzzer, the helmsman would check the board and then he would buzz the officer on watch and request permission to carry on with the next leg of the ZZ.

The *Queen Elizabeth* had the most modern steering gear and gauges to help in steering the ship. One gauge showed the exact angle of the rudder. It was, with care, possible to steer half a degree! In the wheelhouse there were three wheels, two telemotor and one electric. Bad steering problems occured once, when an engineer working on one system had made a bad job, allowing the steering to fail. Fortunately,

the quarter-master on duty was familiar with the lay-out and he by-passed one to the other and, without any trouble, continued with good steering. The men on the bridge were always aware that the rudder might have to be put hard over, causing a serious heel, especially at the end of a voyage, and everything possible was done to prevent this. It was also generally recommended that the automatic pilot should not be used. To change over to manual steering would have cost too much time and, if an emergency should occur, this loss of time could have brought a whole contingent into serious trouble. Zig-zagging, would never allow the auto-pilot to be used. To avoid the auto-pilot getting out of order, it was sometimes tested in quiet water.

In bad weather zig-zagging carried on as long as possible, entirely at the Captain's discretion. It was never necessary to change course very quickly, in these circumstances, but speed was frequently reduced, especially if the safety of the ship and her passengers would be jeopardized.

Submarines experienced difficulties firing torpedoes in heavy weather, for the conning tower could break the surface and be spotted easily. Rolling and pitching became accentuated close to the surface and torpedoes were more difficult to aim. Zig-zagging was only used when you could NOT see a U-boat. If one was sighted the ship would alter course to put it astern and proceed at full speed, or perhaps steer straight at it. To avoid the torpedoes—by altering the course to run parallel with them a ship presents a smaller target.

This is probably what saved the *Queen Elizabeth* from a serious attack, on the afternoon of November 9 1942. A U-boat periscope was sighted by the 6-in gun crew on R-deck aft. It

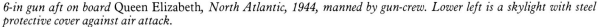

6-in gun aft on board Queen Elizabeth, *North Atlantic, 1944, manned by gun-crew. Lower left is a skylight with steel protective cover against air attack.*

appeared to be *U-704*, under the command of Kapitänleutnant Kessler, in a position roughly 55°N, 29°W. Kessler attacked with a spread of four torpedoes. After two minutes four seconds, Kessler heard an explosion, presumably caused by the self-destructing devices in the topedoes and he was convinced he had scored a hit on the liner. If this were the case then he would have won 250,000 dollars plus the Iron Cross to be awarded by Hitler to the U-boat Captain who could sink one of the *Queens*. Kessler signalled U-Board Command Headquarters in Berlin that he had done so and it was widely announced in the German Press. In America, too, the news was all over New York the following morning.

Most people regarded this event as a great military defeat. However, great was the exuberance a few days later in the Cunard building on November 13, when the *Queen Elizabeth* arrived safely at the Quarantine Base. The incredible thing was that on the ship itself the rumour was not widespread and for many crew members it was more than a surprise to hear and read in the New York papers what had 'actually' happened.

To hit a ship, a U-boat had to fire ahead of it, and so the course and speed had to be known. Hopefully, the zig-zag would confuse the U-boat and thus cause the torpedoes to miss. There were various patterns of zig-zag used on a voyage to prevent U-boats from identifying the zig-zag used and thus make due allowance when spreading torpedoes. As a rule, the more U-boats in the area, the more complicated the zig-zag became.

The *Queen Elizabeth* was sighted by U-boats on many occasions and on the ship it was quite common to receive a radio-message commencing: 'Increased U-boat activity in your vicinity indicates probability that you have been sighted and you should alter course immediately to pass through the following position . . .'

Fog was also often encountered, but the zig-zag pattern had to be maintained. Without this the ship would have made a quicker run. In order not to collide with anything unexpectedly, the *Queen Elizabeth* was fitted out with a radar installation in September 1942 whilst in New York.

The radar was housed in a special shack on the after end of the monkey island. Royal Navy personnel were on board to operate and service this equipment and it was all very 'hush-hush' and out of bounds to all hands, including navigation officers. The type of set was known as an 'A-scan' radar, which carried a distance scale across the central radar tower (CRT). A green- -pip indicated the distance of a target. The bearing of the target was indicated by the angle of the antenna. On receiving a target, the radar operator would telephone the bridge and state that a target was bearing, say Green 060°, which was probably 10 miles distant. The bridge messenger would relay this message to the officer on watch.

There were some problems initially in the interpretation of the bearing, because 'Green 060°' meant 60° to starboard of the ship's head, but what was the ship's head? Time would be lost between the radar operator taking the bearing and the bridge messenger passing the message to the officer on watch and in the meantime, the ship was on a zig-zag! It was doubtful whether the radar would pick up a periscope, but it should pick

Sketch from the crow's nest illustrating much of the ship's armament and central radar tower (CRT) in foreground. Note zig-zag course indicated in top left corner.

up a conning tower and, no doubt, any unidentified targets of similar size ahead. The antenna was swept by a manual control and thus could be kept on one bearing if required. The first types were rather rudimentary. The density of the air was also shown sometimes and this caused a shock occasionally. On many occasions the 'enemy' transpired to be a cold front with a nice shower! Sometimes the radio officers played a part in the handling of the radar installation, but mainly they were to be found in the radio room.

Strict radio silence was maintained, with a continuous listening watch on 500 kHz and continuous monitoring and copying of the naval routines on long-wave and short-wave being transmitted, in code, all the time. When an SOS signal was received this had to be ignored, despite the loss of life involved. Stopping would have meant the ship becoming a sitting duck for any submarine still lurking in the area.

East of 45°W, the ship was under the control of the Admiralty and west of that degree she was controlled by the United States Navy in Washington, who relayed their messages from the Admiralty.

During the war, monitoring stations were set up from the Shetland Islands to North Africa and high frequency direction finding equipment took fixes on submarines' daily radio reports. If a U-boat was 'discovered' lying in wait for a convoy, the U-boat's messages to Berlin were usually intercepted by these monitoring stations. If the U-boat had 'found' an enemy ship her coded messages usually started with 'E.E.'

This code was broken by the Allies and was used in reporting to their vessels about a submarine's position. For this purpose, the *Queen Elizabeth* carried code and cipher tables; the decoding was done by WRNS serving on board. Each day they received some of these messages, but once every day the ship had to be checked regarding her own position as well. Radio silence was broken to receive another coded message, in which the ship's position was mentioned. If there was an hour's difference at the time between real and reported positions, the ship herself had to break silence, to report to the Admiralty.

Weather reports were received uncoded. It was too difficult to change forecasts into coded signals and one had also to bear in mind that there were still neutral ships crossing the Atlantic, also depending on these reports. About every six hours the forecast was sent across and in rough weather it was done every three hours.

Fog and mist did not have too much effect on the ship's movement, but storms could become a real threat.

In February 1944, on her way to New York, the *Queen Elizabeth* was going through very heavy swells, almost hove to, doing about 7 or 8 knots. The ship was being tossed around like a cork. In mountainous seas she was rising up on the crest of one wave, then down in the valley of another one when a tremendous freak wave crashed aboard immediately abaft the windlass capstans. It felt, as if she was heading for the bottom of the ocean. Some 3,000 tons of water had hit the ship, depressing the foredeck by several inches and badly cracking it athwartships, causing great damage to the windlasses and the 3-in gun-scuttles, which were almost torn from their

Winter on the North Atlantic, 1944. Sketched from the monkey island, this drawing shows a typical winter passage in a beam sea.

seatings. Water also reached the decks below, some buckling in many places. A number of stanchions were broken or twisted and heavy sprays smashed several of the wheel-house windows, leaving splinters of glass in the woodpanelling. Some of the glass also severed communication wires whilst water even went down the No 1 funnel.

Immediately below the wheel-house the Staff Captain had his quarters. He was in the act of shaving when an enormous amount of water came into his cabin. One block of plate glass hit him and knocked him down. Fortunately he was uninjured although sitting in water up to his waist! Following this incident the ship had to be taken into dry dock for six weeks. The Bethlehem Steel Company of New Jersey did a most fantastic job in putting her in order again.

Every time she got into New York, extra AA guns were added and within a short time the *Queen Elizabeth* was very heavily armed, guns being piled around the funnels and along the sun deck. Several twin Bofors, rockets and a great number of 20-mm Oerlikons replaced the earlier variety of lighter machine guns such as Vickers, Brownings and .50 calibres, which were all taken ashore. Throughout the ship, miles of extra wiring was installed to handle these guns and connect them with telephone exchanges.

The gun crews were a mixed bunch. The officer in command was a RNVR Lieutenant-Commander and a US Army Artillery Captain was his second-in-command. In total 300 AA ratings would serve in three watches. There were also some Maritime Regiment personnel, who were supplemented by servicemen travelling overseas.

The guns were always manned at sea by the permanent crew, supplemented by the troops on board, and every morning the guns were tested, well away from land of course, causing a tremendous vibration throughout the ship. About every third trip there would also be a General Alarm and all guns would be fired at parachute flares released from the ship.

At the end of each voyage, when nearing the coasts, the number of U-boats in the vicinity was high. Thus a few hundred miles from the coast, the ship would rendezvous with a naval escort,

Top left *The forward deck, from the crow's nest, showing gunners at their post* (Imperial War Museum).
Centre left *British gunners do a spot of practice* (Imperial War Museum).
Left *US gunners carrying out their drill. Note the zig-zag wake* (Imperial War Museum).

mostly consisting of destroyers and cruisers, usually totalling six or seven. Naturally, these vessels could not cope with the speed of the *Queen Elizabeth*, especially in rough seas, so normally the escort would sail ahead of her in the same zig-zag pattern.

This could lead to very dangerous situations, highlighted in the incident where the *Queen Mary* collided with HMS *Curacao*, sinking her. After this incident, naval escorts were reduced for that part of the voyage. Air support was also received from Catalina flying boats and Liberator planes.

On one occasion, in 1943, the vigilance of a Canadian pilot saved the *Queen Elizabeth*. The pilot spotted a U-boat silently concealed in the liner's path. As the aircraft came out of the dark, the U-boat fired and then disappeared. Fortunately the pilot of the plane was able to pass on the U-boat's position to the liner, which had already altered course. Often on the American side 'blimps' were seen carrying out anti-submarine sweeps. They were not real escorts, although they may have been ordered to sweep ahead of the *Queens*.

The German U-boats were certainly far from their home-bases, but they were frequently seen off the American coast. This was often witnessed at tragic intervals by the sinking of many vessels off Sandy Hook, helplessly watched by people on the New Jersey Boardwalk or on the Long Island beaches. Should a mistake in the calculations on when to rendezvous occur, then there was a fair chance of a U-boat waiting in the rendezvous area!

On the British side of the Atlantic the Northern Approach was also full of U-boat activity and depth-charging had to be undertaken very frequently. The tremendous power of these bombs could be felt in the ship, shock waves causing vibrations throughout the whole structure.

All ports were approached along 'swept' channels which were swept as often as possible by trawlers. These channels were often extremely crowded with vessels, as in the Irish Sea, and in these waters the possibility of collision increased although navigation lights were shown at reduced

Top right *British gunners on the alert* (Imperial War Museum).
Centre right *Action Stations for all gun crews!* (Imperial War Museum).
Right *Foredeck with the bow anchor cable in foreground and showing clearly the 3-in guns. Photograph was probably taken in early 1945 since the protective bridge shield has already been removed* (Imperial War Museum).

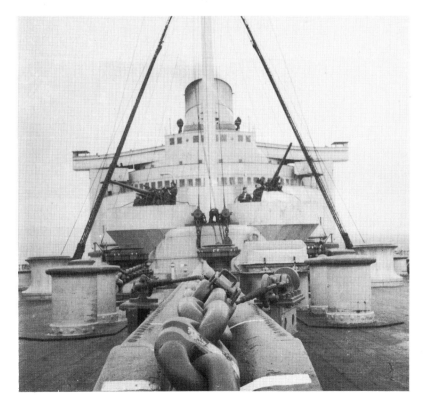

intensity. Throughout the voyage the ship had travelled in complete darkness—ships can be seen without sidelights by watching their wake—and the radar could always be depended on. In bad weather there was far more danger from collision with other vessels than from U-boat attacks and sidelights were often switched on. Switching these lights on in confined coastal waters surprised people—especially when the ship left the Clyde, since the whole of that area was in complete blackout, as protection against bomber attacks—but still it appeared to be safe enough to switch them on when needed. This of course, did not mean that the light could be exposed frequently. All the ship's windows were painted grey, with black on the inside. During fine weather they were often opened to get some fresh air, but all had to be firmly closed again during blackout, this normally being undertaken by the stewards. Blackout lasted from dusk until dawn and the gun crews were all closed up at a state of instant readiness.

Normally Squadron Leader Turnbull (Royal Canadian Air Force), a member of the permanent staff, would make an announcement over the

Above left *Sketch for the original painting made by Oswald Brett, showing the* Queen Elizabeth *making heavy weather on a westbound winter-crossing of the North Atlantic. Painting in possesion of the author.*

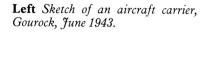

Left *Sketch of an aircraft carrier, Gourock, June 1943.*

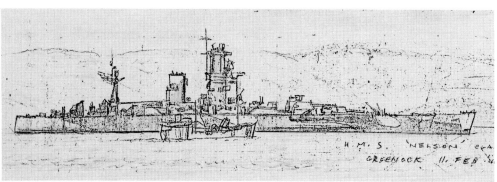

Left HMS Nelson *at Greenock in February 1944.*

Home Visit! At 'The Hole'—her anchorage—being attended by various small supply vessels, including the 'old servant' Romsey (Imperial War Museum).

public-address system to the effect that 'Blackout is now in force till 06:00 hours in the morning. All windows, portholes and doors leading to the open deck must be closed and secured.'

This order was absolutely rigid. No smoking was allowed on deck, nor were you allowed to open a window, porthole or door. Doors leading to the decks had a wooden partition erected around them to form a small room which shielded the open decks from the interior lighting of the ship. This area was painted entirely black with a canvas curtain on it and, as you closed the inside door, you stepped out through a black canvas screen. Inside the partition there was only a small, blue light, giving just enough light to indicate where you were going.

Eastbound trips were all made to Gourock. The reason for choosing the Clyde area was obvious. The terminal British port had to be: (i) a safe anchorage for the ship, despite the weather circumstances, safe from sea and air attacks; (ii) capable of handling a large number of troops in the quickest possible way, once they were landed; and (iii) have excellent railway facilities, as troops after landing had then to be transferred by rail to their various destinations.

The best way to disembark the troops would be to moor alongside a quay, but both possibilities for this were out of the question. Southampton was too near to the enemy. Germany had occupied France, which was well within bomber range, and the city was often heavily attacked. Liverpool also suffered from heavy air raids and was fully occupied with smaller troopships and transports, as well as food and store-ships.

So it was decided that the Clyde would be the best choice. Here was a natural harbour, capable of anchoring well over 100 ships on some

occasions, which was powerfully protected from air and sea attacks by anti-submarine nets and patrols. Also aircraft carriers were frequently there when the *Queen Elizabeth* approached the Firth of Clyde, giving sufficient air support. Gourock was chosen since Princess Pier at Greenock, which would have been the perfect choice, was fully occupied, being part of a naval base. The *Queen Elizabeth* would normally anchor at Tail-of-the-Bank, where she had plenty of room to swing, and her deep water spot for the coming years was known as 'The Hole'.

With no pier available, the troops, their packs and the mailbags, which were usually carried, were brought ashore by pleasure steamers, among which the *King George V* and *King Edward VII* were well known. Two tenders were also used, these being the *Romsey* (the Alexandra Towing Company's fast-tug tender) and the *Rowena* from Belfast. Stores and baggage was handled by Dutch coasters, which had succeeded in escaping from the Netherlands when Germany invaded that country in May 1940. Some of these coasters had already been in British ports when war broke out. Many of these vessels were now working for the British and these became quite famous because of the plants and flowers which they grew in pots in their windows and portholes. Soon the area between Greenock and Gourock became known as 'Rotterdam Bay'!

Whilst the *Queen Elizabeth* was anchored at Gourock, many of the ship's shell doors were opened. A lot of baggage and commodities were handled but security at these doors was not very tight. This was in complete contrast to the situation in New York. There, a US Army company was permanently quartered on the pier and there were always well over a hundred GIs

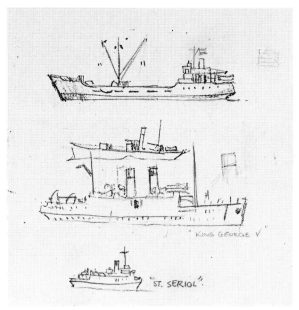

Some vessels which attended the Queen Elizabeth *at Gourock during the war, as sketched in 1943.*

patrolling the area. GIs were on constant duty on gang-ways to check all passes. The British government had consular security officers who patrolled the ship whilst in port. As far as the *Queen Elizabeth* was concerned, there was one on

duty throughout. The officer worked an eight hour shift. These officers also visited other ships. No one was allowed to smoke on open decks; the GIs in New York would forcibly stop anyone defying this order—the *Normandie* was still there! On one occasion the Senior Third Officer and the Senior First Officer were on station at the stern on arrival in New York. The time from taking the shore line until the berthing operation was finally completed, was usually about half an hour, though before this period had elapsed GIs would already be patrolling the ship. The Senior First said, 'I have just time for a cigarette before the patrol reaches here' and immediately lit up. He had only taken a couple of puffs before the mooring was finished and he thought he had better extinguish the cigarette, in order to set a good example to the crew. He extinguished the cigarette, but left it between his fingers. This was soon noticed by a patrolling GI who politely but firmly told him to stop smoking.

At the ship's main fire station a special direct telephone had been connected to the New York Fire Department, and this was manned by an American Fire Brigade officer. In the event of an alarm sounding, this officer had to pick up the receiver and say that an alarm had sounded. Three fire-engines would be despatched immediately, even if it was a false alarm!

Chapter 7

Eastbound—troops for the front

Eastbound Voyages were all recorded as AT Convoys (AT standing for Army Transport).

To embark 15,000 troops without good planning would most certainly have resulted in chaos. Most of them had no idea of what it was like to be aboard a ship. The Captain and Staff Captain were very much responsible for this planning. An advance party was needed to come on board some two days prior to the ship's departure, consisting of 2,000 men, to decide on the quartering of the various units of troops throughout the voyage. Included in this advance party were Military Police, sentries, guides, kitchen porters, cooks, butchers, mess orderlies, anti-submarine look-outs and gunners. The advance party prepared for and helped out during the voyage and were the liaison between the troops and the crew. Once on board there would be much consultation between the advance party, the Troop Office and the ship's Second Officer.

Normally the ship started to embark the troops at 7:00 pm. Most of these men appeared a little arrogant, provincial and incredibly naive regarding the rest of the world outside the USA. They envisaged this as barbarous or hopelessly primitive territory—'They would show the Germans what was what—and would be back in good old US of A in six months or so.' Of course it did not work out that way for many of them and those who were fortunate enough to return were certainly far more realistic in their outlook. Of course there were exceptions to the general ignorance, and many of the men were well informed about Europe and more than eager to learn about conditions outside their home country. Many of the troops had to travel days before arriving at this final assembly point, whilst others had been waiting in line all day to embark. They arrived from their camps up-river by ferry or train and they were 'unloaded' in special formations, before being marched on board. A

general view of this mass of men, waiting to board the ship, gave the impression of looking down on a bed of mushrooms.

Each man had to call out his name as he boarded and filed past the embarkation desks, being then handed a coloured tag to remind him of his mealtimes, his bunk number and his muster-station location. Once on board the men were directed by guides to their quarters and were instructed to remain there until the embarkation was completed. Usually this took about six hours, by which time the men were feeling so tired that they were more than glad to turn in and get some much needed sleep. The first morning after embarkation, still alongside the pier, the military officers were called to a detailed briefing given by the Staff Captain and the OC Troops. Here the ship's routine, the various drills (emergency, air-raid), blackout, cleanliness of quarters and the procedures of abandoning ship, was explained.

The officers were then responsible for transmitting this information back to the men in their command. Discipline was very strict and absolutely no distinctions were made between officers and men breaking the regulations.

Troops had their own way of handling discipline on the ship and at certain points they had someone on guard duty, who was not armed but who just stood there, wearing his life-jacket. Alley-ways, deck-squares, mess-rooms and quarters were controlled in that way, and the guards themselves were supervised by an officer.

A Sergeant of the guards, assigned to guard-duty with orders to see that there was no smoking or lights on the open decks after sunset and that nothing was thrown overboard, recalls: 'We posted our guards on two watches, except for one post in the belly of the ship. The air was so foul and the area was so claustrophobic that this guard had to be relieved every half hour. Women's quarters were off limits to male personnel and some guards were posted in the corridors there, but even this did not seem to be very effective. There nearly was a riot one night, when I took nearly thirty half-frozen deck-guards to the galley in the small hours of the morning and the galley staff refused them a hot drink and sandwiches.'

Standing orders were given, very clearly and rigidly, as follows: 'All orders will be issued in the spirit that this ship is engaged in a combined operation of war, requiring full loyalty, obedience and co-operation from all personnel on board'

The washing of laundry is prohibited. Personnel will not climb in the ship's rigging, sit on the railings, life-rafts, or climb into the life-boats. With both feet on deck you cannot fall overboard. If anyone falls overboard IT WILL BE IMPOSSIBLE TO STOP THE SHIP FOR RECOVERY PURPOSES.'

'The ship will be very crowded. The exigencies of the times demand it. Officers and men should not view this trip as a vacation: it will be anything but that.

'Radio sets, electric razors, electric phonographs, flashlights, electric irons, knives usable as weapons and cameras are forbidden.

'As long as the ship floats, your best place is on board. Have your life-jacket properly adjusted. It will support you for a very long time. There are ample ladders, scramble nets and knotted ropes to allow everyone to enter the water without jumping—and go for a raft!

'Smoking is prohibited in cabins, troop compartments and corridors at all times.'

'Gambling, profane or obscene language and all unnecessary noises are also prohibited. Intoxicants are prohibited. This is a dry ship.'

Even the correct dress for the voyage was a part of the rules and regulations: 'Enlisted men will wear fatigues unless specifically stated otherwise; officers will wear shirts and ties [and], blouses, if available, during the evening meal.'

When darkness fell, some 24 hours after embarkation had started, the ship departed. Leaving during these hours of darkness had two

Evening over Manhattan, June 1944.

main reasons. First it reduced the number of people on the pier watching the ship's departure. If this were too public an event then no one could be sure that her departure was not reported to the enemy. Second, slipping away in the darkness was also regarded to be safer for dropping the pilot at Sandy Hook as, when this occurred, by necessity the vessel came almost to a stand-still and would have made a perfect target.

It was not always possible to wait until darkness. On many occasions she had to leave by daylight to catch the tide. For those on board a moment they would never forget. As the giant ship gently moved down the river towards Verrazano Narrows and the open sea, she passed that grand old lady, The Statue of Liberty, with her right hand and her torch held high. With one question foremost in their minds: 'Will we ever see her again?', there were many whose eyes felt

Right *Statue of Liberty from* Queen Elizabeth *in 1943.*
Below *Battery Point, New York. An amateur photographer makes a fine shot of the vessel as the* Queen Elizabeth *leaves for Scotland* (Chris Konings collection).

the emotion of the moment. Naval patrol planes, such as Kingfisher (Curtiss), Goose (Gruman) and Mariners (Martin) escorted the ship then until darkness.

The first air-raid drills were started even as the ship made her way down the Hudson. When these drills took place every man had to go below decks to take cover in his quarters. Lifeboat drill was to follow and everyone had to muster on the boat deck and promenade deck. At this first lifeboat drill some of the crew were lined up as 'volunteers' to start the lifeboat engines. The men chosen then had to step into the lifeboats, a distance of two feet. This proved quite a frightening experience for some of the 'volunteers', viewing the water from such a height rushing by down below them, to such an extent that some of them never again appeared at lifeboat drill!

The only personnel exempt from attending the drills were gunners, anti-submarine lookouts, mess orderlies, kitchen helpers and the 'Sweeping Parties'. These men were recruited to help the crew run the ship and to keep it in good order and in a healthy condition, and consisted of 340 mess orderlies, 1,200 police, 60 mess-hall cleaners, 40 store carriers, 300 AA gun parties, 70 potato peelers, 300 stairway cleaners and 200 spare men. All of these men were simply detailed by their quarters. Since it was impossible to obtain genuine 'volunteers', these jobs were designated by quarters, ie, one would automatically fill the job of mess orderly when one was sleeping in, for instance, a cabin on D deck. At first these extra

Above *An aerial view of 'boat drill' whilst travelling at 28½ knots!* (US National Archives).

Below *Troops in the mess hall, later to be the first class dining room* (University Archives, University of Liverpool).

Right *Menu card produced for the Christmas dinner on December 25 1945.*

helpers were not too happy about the situation until alerted by the ship's crew that these extra duties also carried extra privileges—fresh-water showers in the crew's quarters, free meals all day through, ice cream, etc. Now people were eager to help, as wearing a white apron meant that you were no longer confined to your special area in the ship, but could walk freely anywhere you liked.

During the early hours of the voyage, the Captain addressed the troops over the public-address system to the effect that the use of the ship was part of Britain's 'reverse lease-lend programme' and that it would take more than one torpedo to sink her. Above all, he mentioned that the ship was British and actually made in Scotland. Many of the Americans found this fact very difficult to comprehend as they believed that only the USA was capable of building a vessel of this size. Quite a number of them, too, thought the Captain's words to be British propaganda!

A major problem for the organisers was how to see that this great 'guest' was never hungry! To serve 15,000 troops with enough food for about six days, two meals were organised, each lasting for six setings.

Breakfast started as 06:30 hours and lasted until 11:00 hours, with 45-minute intervals. Tea started at 15:00 hours and lasted until 19:30 hours. The number shown on the tag corresponded with the mess sitting, which was announced over the public address system as follows: 'This is the sixth and last call for the troop's mess hall. All troops with No 6 mess-card, FORM YOUR LINE.'

When entering the mess hall each man had to show his tag, before he could proceed further. The troops only brought their mug, spoon, knife and fork as they walked along in two lines which were controlled by MPs. Messing officers and stewards directed them to their seats and the troops would fill the tables to rated capacity so that there were places for everyone. They remained seated, as their food was brought by mess orderlies from the galley in flat trays which were heated in hot presses.

The saying 'God sends the food and the Devil sends the cook' was not really appropriate for the *Queen Elizabeth*, though many troops agreed with the expression. Many of them were seasick and without appetite, but those who were not were fed with edible food — certainly not gourmet standard, food which was plain but at least good.

CANADIAN ARMY OVERSEAS

CHRISTMAS
DINNER

at Sea

25 DECEMBER, 1945

Aboard

H.M.T. QUEEN ELIZABETH

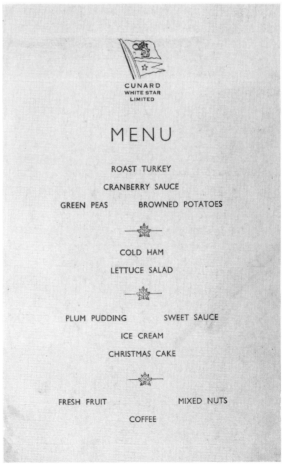

CUNARD
WHITE STAR
LIMITED

MENU

ROAST TURKEY

CRANBERRY SAUCE

GREEN PEAS   BROWNED POTATOES

COLD HAM

LETTUCE SALAD

PLUM PUDDING   SWEET SAUCE

ICE CREAM

CHRISTMAS CAKE

FRESH FRUIT   MIXED NUTS

COFFEE

In bad weather the number of troops in the 'chow line' went down drastically. Many tables were available then and for the remaining troops it was amusing to see the mess gear sliding up and down the narrow tables; one never knew for sure whether one was eating from one's own gear or from someone else's! The officers dined differently, however, and in a report on a voyage in 1943, the ship's chef was complimented for the way he prepared and attractively served his food.

As soon as the troops had finished their meal, they got up, emptied their food refuse into garbage pans at the end of the tables and then proceeded to the aft end of the mess hall, to avoid 'traffic jams' with those who were already waiting and queuing for the next sitting.

Taking their mess-kits with them, the troops left the hall in six lines, two through each of the three exits, routed by MPs to the kit-washers, where they walked by a vat conataining hot salt water, dipped their dish in this and then proceeded to a further vat, this time holding hot soapy, salt water for a further dip. The soap used in this vat was of a nonlather type, so that only odd suds were visible. They finally dipped their dish in a vat of clear, fresh water, for a final rinse, before returning to their quarters. It was a cause of amusement to see the troops, walking along the decks, shaking the water off their mess-gear, in an attempt to dry these off before stowing them away, ready for the next meal.

Since there were only two meals served a day, the men were allowed to eat as much as they could and to give some idea of what was required to serve all these people during one voyage, hereunder is only part of the 'shopping list':

  76,000 lbs of flour and cereals
  21,500 lbs of bacon and hams
155,000 lbs of meat and poultry
  4,600 lbs of cheese
18,000 lbs of jams
31,000 lbs of canned meals
29,000 lbs of fresh fruit
31,000 lbs of sugar, tea, coffee
53,600 lbs of butter, eggs, milk powder
124,300 lbs of potatoes

For the Jewish people on board a special kosher food store was provided.

England was still rationed during these years, but America could provide anything and everything. Many of the above items were stored in New York for the return voyage as well. It was impossible to take on board the vast amount of bread which would be consumed so, for the first few days of each voyage, bread was used which

A very rare photograph showing the Queen Elizabeth *in heavy weather, taken from a US escorting aircraft contrary to regulations and later printed on board in the ship's printing shop.*

had been baked and bought in New York. Meanwhile, the bakery on board was working 24 hours a day, preparing and baking all varieties of rolls, loaves, etc, to be eaten on the remainder of the voyage. A vast amount of meat also had to be prepared and slicing machines worked continuously throughout the whole of the voyage. Chickens also had a busy time, producing 30,000 eggs a day, to be boiled for breakfast.

Between these mealtimes, the troops had very little to do apart from walking the decks and sleeping, interspersed only with life-jacket and drill parades. The monotony of this situation soon gave rise to frustration and boredom, so the 'powers that be' had to give considerable attention to ways of keeping the men occupied and entertained. For this purpose, films were shown on the promenade deck, since the theatre had now become troop accommodation. The operation to convert the promenade deck into a cinema was quite simple and proved to be very practicable. All the windows were closed, thus providing a blackout from one side to the other and to the aft enclosed section abreast of the No 2 funnel. The screen was sited somewhere near the stairway at the after end, and the troops thus had to stand forward, near to the projector.

Lectures were given on the British way of life and for this purpose the troops were supplied with an issue of *A short guide to Great Britain*, prepared by the Special Services Division, Army Service Forces United States Army, and published by the War and Navy Department, Washington.

Advice on 'The country', 'English versus

American language', 'Some important do's and don'ts were among the chapters and below is an extract from this publication:

'Don't be a show off! The British dislike bragging and showing off!

'The British are tough! Don't be misled by the British tendency to be soft-spoken and polite. If they need to be, they can be pretty tough. The English language didn't spread across the oceans and over the mountains, jungles and swamps of the world because these people were panty-waist. 'You can rub a Britisher the wrong way by telling him "We came over and won the last one!" Each nation did its share, but the British remember that nearly a million of their best manhood died in the last war. Such arguments are dead issues. Nazi-propaganda now is pounding away day and night.

'A British woman officer or non-commissioned officer can—and often does—give orders to a man Private. They have stuck to their posts near burning ammunition depots, delivered messages afoot after motor cycles have been blasted under them. When you see a girl in Khaki or air-force blue with a bit of ribbon on her tunic—remember she didn't get it for knitting more socks than anyone else in Ipswich!

'NEVER criticize the King or the Queen.

'Use common-sense on all occasions.

'It is always impolite to criticize your hosts, and it's militarily stupid to criticize your Allies!'

Officers were also given lectures and advice on how much to tip the Cunard steward for their services; a single American officer would pay $1.00 to the Bedroom Steward and the Table Steward and a British Major payed 5/-, when he was single and 7/6d when he was married.

There were also phrase books issued as practical aids for the troops, for example, when asking questions on vital matters, repairs to vehicles, enemy strength, weapons, wounded, etc. If you were in need of some lighter reading, small novels were also issued, as were pocket-books published by the War Department, some containing historical information and others giving summaries of the works of various British authors.

Occasionally concerts were held in the lounge and some of these were very memorable. On one occasion both James Cagney and Irving Berlin were travelling on board. While Berlin played his well known tunes on the piano, some of the naval personnel accompanied him on their own instruments, whilst a chorus was formed of both naval personnel and American troops—all wonderful fun and Berlin certainly knew how to

get them all in the mood. Cagney, likewise, spent time wandering around amongst the crew, chatting and laughing with them at will—certainly a big boost to the morale of all those on board. On other occasions, Edward G. Robinson and Douglas Fairbanks Jnr also travelled across on the *Queen Elizabeth*, and again gave a boost to all those travel-weary troops.

Glenn Miller's Band really turned the June 21 1944 crossing from a cramped week-long traffic jam of people into something faintly approaching an MGM musical. They played every day in the main lounge and once or twice on deck and they were very, very good. The band was made up of the best professional musicians in the service and they had lots of 'perks' but thay paid the country back with enthusiasm, playing the popular Glenn Miller hits of that time, like *In the Mood, Kalamazoo*, and of course *Moonlight Serenade.* Glenn Miller himself was not aboard. He had crossed earlier by air and met his band via a tender at Greenock.

Church services were also held on board at regular intervals, organised by the Padres and Red Cross Officers, and these were always well attended.

German phrase book issued to troops as an aid when dealing with vital matters.

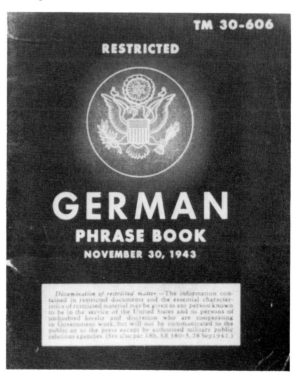

Certainly more popular though than this, the most actively enjoyed pastime of all GIs was gambling. The playing of the game Parchesi had become very popular. To many people this had been a 'dumpy' game, but early in 1942 it was streamlined and played with dice. Some of the tournaments could continue for several days, such was the GIs involvement. When the black troops were gambling, before a throw of the dice, they would shake their dice beside an ear and say, 'speak to me bones'!

Another popular game was poker. All these games of chance required money, of course and, whilst the US troops were well paid compared with the British, they still lost quite a lot of their earnings. However, there was always a way for some of the men to make extra money, if they so

wished. Twelve hours between two mealtimes was a long time, during which most of the men became hungry. To cater for this on board were several canteens, either PXs for the Americans or NAAFIs for the British. Cigarettes, Coca-cola, chocolate, candy bars, razor blades and magazines could be bought there. Many of the gamblers became so engrossed in their game that they had neither the time nor the inclination to make that long walk down the stairs into the unhealthy atmosphere, where all the windows were closed and where there was no proper air-conditioning (although that was ingeniously enlarged and overhauled), to buy their own refreshments, The enterprising ones took matters into their own hands, purchased the refreshments from the canteens and then went

Americans preferred to relax over a game of dice, but didn't take chances otherwise—note life-preservers (Mae Wests!) (Imperial War Museum).

back and re-sold these—at a profit, of course—to the ardent gamblers. (American enterprise at its best!)

Despite all official efforts to create entertainment and interesting pastimes, the troops were still bored. They certainly had no enthusiasm for the war and openly expressed their wish to be back home. Who could blame them? Many would walk round and round the decks, others would just sit, looking sadly at the sea, while others, with more enthusiasm, would try to carve their initials in the teak-wood railings of the ship.

And, as can be imagined, 15,000 troops can

Right *Oerlikon gun position below port wing of bridge—a very cold early morning, looking aft from the crow's nest. Probably late October 1944 in the Irish Sea off the south-east coast of Ireland.*

Below *3-in high-angle and low-angle gun on starboard foredeck of* Queen Elizabeth, *September 1944, as sketched from the crow's nest. The notation on sketch is as follows: 'GIs bound overseas, unglamorous transport life.'*

WAR DEPARTMENT PAMPHLET NO. 21-15

YOU DON'T THINK...

certainly make a mess of one big luxury liner! Not only were they careless with the ship and its fixtures and fittings, they were also careless regarding their personal hygiene. Because there was insufficient fresh water in ship's tanks on board, the showers were changed into salt water ones with a special soap to be used with them. However, these proved most unpopular with the result that many of the troops didn't bother to shower frequently! In contrast, despite their cramped facilities most officers still had the use of a bath.

For their future health, the War Department supplied a booklet advising how to prevent getting VD. These booklets, together with many of the other issues supplied to them, were found

Left *'You Don't Think . . .' booklet issued to troops to tell them about the dangers of VD.*
Below *The knighthead lookout. A wet morning, April 1945, Firth of Clyde. Note the telegraphs used to receive mooring and anchoring instructions from the bridge and the foc'sle head bell which was stowed in the 'fog locker' under the knighthead when leaving port. When at anchor the bell was struck once for each 15 fathoms of cable let go.*

Vessels at anchor in the Firth of Clyde ready for convoy assembly, October 1944.

scattered all over the ship. The GIs were so careless with their belongings, even weapons, that a whole British battalion could have been kitted out with what the Americans left behind on the ship! Blankets, used by those who slept on the open decks in the summer, were used for years afterwards in the homes of some of the crew members. One crew member still uses a razor he bought from an Irish dayman who found it on the ship.

The enormous amount of rubbish, such as cartons, lolly papers, biscuit packages and the garbage collected from the kitchens and dining-rooms, was disposed of at midnight, every night, often taking three to four hours to dump all the stuff over the side. This operation had to be undertaken during the hours of darkness for, in the daytime, a trail of rubbish could be spotted by an enemy plane. The timing of this meant that, by the time dawn came, the *Queen Elizabeth* would be well away from it and probably most of the waste would have been sunk or dispersed by the sea.

After about six days at sea the troops would welcome the sight of flocks of seagulls, wheeling over their heads. This sight was soon to be followed by an even more welcoming picture—that of escorting ships and aircraft coming out to meet them. A few hours later, the tall rock of Ailsa Craig would loom before them and this was the final indication that the journey was almost at an end. As soon as disembarkation was completed the troops were despatched immediately to different locations throughout England, soon to become part of the cruel battles still raging in Europe.

They took with them, though, many impressions and memories of the huge creature which had had the incredible task of transporting them from their homelands, thousands of miles across the ocean, to bring them to these battlefields of Europe. It was certainly an experience that they would never forget.

The *Queen Elizabeth* did not only carry troops on her eastbound voyages but very often a varied complement of other passengers—diplomats, high ranking service personnel, professional people who had been working in the States, and even the ordinary 'man in the street' who had to return to the UK for personal reasons.

One Irishman, returning to the UK for professional reasons, recalls that the Cunard office at 25 Broadway informed him that he was too late for the sailing of the *Aquitania*, so they were booking him a passage on the next ship sailing, the *Queen Elizabeth*. This gentleman

ELIZABETHAN NEWS

Publishing Address: BRITISH LIAISON STAFF OFFICE, "A" DECK SQUARE

SERIES 4, No. 5 TUESDAY, NOVEMBER 3, 1942 TWO CENTS

NEW TACTICS IN DESERT WAR

ARTILLERY BARRAGE

The Eighth Army renewed its attacks against the Axis forces in the Egyptian desert, and made a new advance in the coast region. The British troops maintained the pressure against strong German and Italian opposition, repulsing heavy counter-attacks.

"_The task of reducing the enemy defences may be a very long one,_" states an official communique from Cairo, "_But our infantry are slowly nibbling their way forward._"

The new Allied method of attack is a very heavy artillery barrage with infantry, supported by tanks, held in readiness to force a break-through.

Attack Repulsed

Enemy infantry, followed by tanks, made an attack on the British right flank in the sector between the coastal railway and the coast. The attack was repulsed and many prisoners were taken.

Dive-Bomber Raid

In a German dive-bombing attack, seven _Stukas_ were destroyed and many others severely damaged. The enemy, in his haste to escape the British fighters, jettisoned bombs on his own lines.

BRITAIN'S SHIPPING AND WAR SUPPLIES RECORD

The Minister of Home Security, Mr. Herbert Morrison, in a speech in London yesterday, gave some striking facts on the British achievement in making and shipping war supplies.

Out of every 200 ships convoyed, he said, 199 of them had been brought safely to port.

Axis Shipping Losses

Remarking on heavy Axis shipping losses, he stated that over 125 enemy warships had been destroyed, captured or damaged, and that well over 6,000,000 tons of shipping had suffered the same fate.

Of the home front, Mr. Morrison declared that over 80 per cent. of all production in Britain had been shipped overseas.

R.A.F. SWEEP OVER FRANCE

In raids over northern France yesterday, Bostons heavily bombed and machine-gunned factories, freight-yards, airdromes and railway stations.

Holland Attacked

Later in the day, a number of targets in Holland were attacked.

AUSTRALIAN FLIERS IN RUSSIA

Australian airmen have been operating in Russia for some time, it was revealed yesterday. Their task has been the protection of convoys bound for Murmansk.

In the South-West Pacific

ALLIED PLANES BATTER JAPANESE WARSHIPS

Series of Terrific Air Blows

The Japanese have suffered serious losses in a series of terrific blows by Allied air forces in the south-west Pacific, according to despatches from the battle zones.

In raids on the Stewart Islands, two aircraft carriers were damaged, two battleships bombed and three cruisers hit, while over 100 planes were destroyed and probably 50 more damaged.

Australian-based bombers, in raids on Buin and Rabaul last week, scored two hits on battleships, destroyed a heavy cruiser, which blew up, and damaged two light cruisers. Three freighters were hit, another destroyed, and several others damaged.

Another Carrier Sunk

A later report states that Japan has last another aircraft carrier, the sixth since the war in the Pacific commenced.

GUADALCANAL DEFENDERS STRIKE AT JAPANESE

Guadalcanal's defenders struck at the Japanese in combined land, sea and air attacks. United States warships shelled enemy shore positions.

NEW STALINGRAD ATTACKS HELD

Renewed German attacks on the factory area in Stalingrad have been fought to a stand-still. In some instances, the Russians have advanced after capturing a number of German strong-points.

During the last twenty-four hours, German air units have maintained a systematic bombing of the area.

Pravda stated yesterday that the Nazi onslaught in Stalingrad had only brought them fresh casualties and no gains.

Nalchik Situation Grave

Moscow admitted yesterday that the situation in Nalchik was grave.

Russian forces have fallen back to new defensive positions.

In the Ukraine, Russian guerrillas derailed five German military trains and killed many officers and men.

U.S. EXPERTS SEE 1943 PLANES

United States experts visiting Britain saw some of the 1943 secret aircraft yesterday.

It is said they will be superior to anything at present in operation. Their speed, armament and bomb-carrying capacity will be greater.

American planes now in production are reported to be of a similar nature.

Large-scale invasion exercises were carried out by United States troops yesterday. The protection of the port was also tested.

"POLICE HAVE SUSTAINED HEAVY LOSSES"

—French Chief's Statement

The Chief of the French Police has issued the following statement in Paris, according to Vichy Radio: "Since October 13, the French police have started to conduct a large-scale campaign against certain dangerous elements. Large stores of explosives, arms and other destructive weapons have been discovered in French homes.

"The police have sustained some heavy losses, yet their task is far from being accomplished."

ODDS AND ENDS—continued

ing to sleep. They must be awake when the ship, already termed the "monarch" by the girls, pulled out from port.

Came the morning: "Tonight's the night, they had to take on a few more troops. Tonight at 11 o'clock—just watch now!"

Next morning: A quick peek through the porthole, and a few hundred feet away there still remained the smoke, the old buildings and all the characteristics of that same port.

Another morning: Whisht! out of bed in a hurry went the C.W.A.C.s. By this time, they knew the motion of the ship in dock, and this was a different feeling. Out the porthole again and—so near and yet so far—there still remained the port.

Yet another morning: A tremor unusual to what we had experienced was felt and finally the ship pushed out to new worlds.

Up on the decks went the C.W.A.C.s. "Goodbye, Canada, we'll be back." And so off to sea went 109 of the Dominion's daughters. Not pleasure bent or on a luxury cruise but as soldiers of Canada's Army to fill important jobs in Canada's overseas war machine.

PATRICIA CONNOLLEY.

ODDS AND ENDS
*
WAR-TIME BRITAIN

Highly unofficial tips on what's what in war-time Britain, as dispensed _en route_ by the old-timers to the biggest R.C.A.F. draft:

BEER: Very, very weak, but still tasty. Liquor: Scarce but not too expensive when you can find it. Pubs: Cheerful, friendly spots.

FOOD: Plentiful but a bit monotonous till you get used to it. You'll miss eggs and fruit at first, and you'll get pretty tired of Brussels sprouts before the Spring. But soon you won't be able to tell the difference between butter and margarine, and if you're living on station you'll be eating a lot better than the average British civilian. Restaurant prices are pegged at a top price of five shillings, and you don't need ration cards for them.

SMOKES: Cigarettes scarce, rather expensive and of war-time quality. Matches very scarce; plenty of lighter fluid and flints, but lighters very expensive and not so good. Hang on to your Ronson.

SHOWS: Theatres booming in London, and plenty of recently-released Hollywood pictures everywhere, but prices somewhat high. If you're on leave in London, go to the Beaver Club, any service canteens or the Overseas League Club for advice on entertainment.

TRAVEL: Not so good. Big signs in railway stations ask: "Is your journey really necessary?" If it isn't, don't make it. Trains are usually crowded, with s.r.o. signs hung out.

CLOTHES: There's a scarcity. Officers get ration coupons, airmen don't. Better not buy anything unless you need it badly.

BLACK-OUT: Everywhere, every night. You can smoke, or use a dimmed flashlight except when there's an Alert.

MONEY: Not so hard to get used to. Remember that a quid's a pound, a bob's a shilling and that it's easy for the newcomer to confuse a two-shilling and two-and-six coin.

PEOPLE: Swell, and very hospitable. Don't take advantage of their generosity. If you accept an invitation to a meal, remember it comes out of the family's rations. Try to take along something from a parcel from home.

THE C.W.A.C.s EMBARK

"Everyone put your luggage out in the corridor immediately" was the stern command. The hearts of 109 Canadian Women's Army Corps personnel gave a terrific thump as they dashed speedily to re-pack for the umpteenth time.

"No," they thought, "it's a snare and a delusion, but we'll play their little game."

Within ten minutes, three hundred duffle bags lay in a tremendous mound in the centre corridor of the C.W.A.C. Training Centre. Trucks arrived and off went the luggage.

"The game is getting a little more difficult" thought the 109 C.W.A.C's.

It was just four o'clock next morning. Dawn had definitely not yet hovered over the horizon; it was pouring with rain.

The girls all scrambled quickly from their beds. In short order they gobbled a rapid breakfast and were all set for further developments. They had a feeling this MUST surely be the big day. That after a month of waiting, false alarms, and of being C.B.d, "B" Company. C.W.A.C., must at last be on its way to England-by-the-sea.

At six o'clock, in full marching order, complete with steel helmets, respirators, capes, gas masks and water bottles, the first large group of women soldiers to set off for an overseas war, paraded quietly through the streets to their train. A day and a night on the train. Then a Canadian port and "our" ship.

Excitement and rumour were rife as the C.W.A.C.s paraded up the gangway. "We'll be there by——" came the word. Came the night. It was no use try-

(Continued in next column)

shared a cabin with a Frenchman who was returning from a lecture tour in Canada. The latter had been imprisoned by the Germans early in the Occupation and, during his time in prison, he said he expected to be brought out and shot any day. Now he was in a situation where he was expecting to be torpedoed any day!

Their cabin, like the majority of others for civilian occupation, was very sparsely furnished and, apart from this and the mess hall during meal times, the only other places available for sitting and relaxing were on the decks.

The same Irishman remembers that there were some thirty civilians travelling, all of whom seemed to be located in cabins within the same area. Sir Thomas Beecham, conductor of the London Philharmonic Orchestra was also on board but, as he was rarely seen in public, it was felt that he was probably quartered in some of the more luxurious accommodation which was still available.

Our Irish friend also recalls that after about two days on board the weather became warmer, an indication that the vessel was routed a long way south. Contact between passengers and the troops was allowed, with the exception of the VIPs and anyone engaged in security work. These were effectively left to their own devices.

As with the troops, the civilians also found little in the way of entertainment or diversion throughout the voyage. One could listen to the radio for the news, or read the ship's newspaper which was issued from the printer's shop. They found interest, too, in wandering around the ship envisaging the intended use of some of the palatial rooms, an indication of the high quality of life which had been planned aboard this vessel prior to the days of wartime service. Even the words 'Midland Bank' in large letters over one of the doors was a reminder of the excellence of the facilities offered to peacetime passengers.

Originally designed as a luxury liner, the *Queen Elizabeth* was also built with the idea of carrying large quantities of mail-bags quickly across the Atlantic. As yet no airmail service had been established over this route, so the mail-bag service aboard the *Queen* was carried on throughout the war, carrying not only thousands of mail-bags for American, Canadian and British forces, but also for the civilian populations of America and the UK. On eastbound voyages, she also carried cargo of food up to 1,000 tons usually, to help combat intense food rationing in the UK. Military goods,

Left *Ship's newspaper published by the British liaison staff office on A deck.*

which were also desperately needed, were also sent over.

Periodically the vessel was officially inspected to see whether further improvements or changes were needed. In May 1943, the *Queen Elizabeth* was visited by a group of US Congressmen, who watched the embarkation of American troops in New York.

Captain Fall, the Master of the vessel, in his welcome speech said: 'I am very happy to have the honour of addressing you, representatives of Congress of this great nation, especially at such a time in our world's history and from my position as commanding the greatest and fastest merchant vessel in the world.

'I am indeed very proud of the ship's achievements. When she made her famous run across the Atlantic during March 1940, everyone imagined she would remain moored up here until the end of hostilities. Of course, as you know it turned out very much the reverse. Since she departed from New York in November 1940, and commenced this work, she has steamed about 230,000 miles equalling nearly eleven times around the world at the Equator, and has carried well over 200,000 military and naval personnel of all the Allied nations, in addition to roughly 18,000 prisoners of war. All this has been done without the loss of one single life.

'The running of this vessel, under these wartime conditions, calls for organisation of the highest order. If you can, imagine me as a form of mayor of an ordinary-sized town or city, the difference being that this floating town or city has to be navigated through fair weather and storms, clear weather and fog, and also, if necessary, fight defensive actions against the enemy.

'I am provided with a Staff Captain, an experienced Ship's Master, together with staff who work in co-ordination with the military, naval, air force, medical and hospital staffs on board.

'The heads of all departments, deck, engineering and catering, all play their part to the full to ensure the smooth running of everything. I could not even begin to tell you of the thousand and one things that crop up in the course of a passage. I can assure you that the assistance of the American military authorities and staffs, both in embarkation and disembarkation, has been of a very high order. Also the assistance given us by your military security personnel and naval staff has been invaluable.

'We have been proud to carry many thousands of your American boys, both across the Atlantic and the Pacific, in this ship, and their good behaviour and good discipline has given us the greatest respect and admiration for them, and I can assure you that they are second to none as, of course, has been proved recently in all the theatres of war.

'When I look back on the position of Great Britain in 1940, when there seemed to us British that no silver lining was visible in the black clouds and when I myself joined up in the Home Guard when on vacation, all we had was a rifle between three men and five rounds of ammunition, guarding the road-blocks. Then came Pearl Harbor, that crushing and treacherous blow of the Japs. Compare those times with the present.

'We are defeating the enemy whilst we are preparing for peace and I marvel at the grit and determination of the English-speaking nations and all our other Allies.

'Nothing can stop us now until the unconditional surrender of the enemy.'

Chapter 8

Westbound—an abandoned ship!

On the return trips to New York or Halifax, the *Queen Elizabeth* had the appearance of a deserted ship. The number of people carried was far less than on the eastbound voyage and for most of the time consisted of RAF personnel, going for training in America or Canada, and RN personnel, most of whom were going to join ships which were due to go into service on the Atlantic run. Others were being transported for training in the USA and Canada. A large number of civilians was also carried, including businessmen, trading between the USA and Canada and Europe, some of whom were accompanied by their families. Others were experts in their own field, oil, transportation, aviation, etc,—who had been sent to boost the war efforts in Europe and who were now returning home either for good of just for a leave period. Many journalists were also carried, frequently those who had been covering the news on the battlefronts and who were now being repatriated for a rest period.

Diplomats and politicians involved in the immense negotiations over problems associated with the war were also frequent travellers on the westbound voyages.

RN and RAF officers proceeding to the USA were given much information concerning this country, even before joining the ship.

Money: Officers could embark on board their transport with a maximum of £10.

Arriving: All transports were met by the British Naval Liaison Officer, in New York or his representative, and officers were at once dispatched to the Barbizon Plaza Hotel, where accommodation for their first night ashore was provided.

Climate: Information was given on what climate to expect in the northern part of the US and in the Gulf of Mexico. Therefore, various advice on clothing was also given.

Clothing: Officers appointed to ships under construction or refit who were likely to be there during the summer months, would require whites and tropical rig, whilst in winter, when it would be very cold, great-coats and other items of extra-warm clothing were recommended. Officers appointed to the permanent staff should bring whites, though khaki uniform was almost universally adopted. They also had to wear brown shoes.

Cost of living: Officers were given some idea of how expensive America was compared to Britain, where prices were much lower. Items mentioned were: hotel rooms, meals, tobacco, cigarettes, laundry (which was very expensive in the USA), Taxis etc.

Mail: Airmail letters to the USA took up to eighteen days and were seldom quicker than surface mail. Ordinary mail took up to a month. Officers had to be aware of this and mail to Britain was equally uncertain.

Since these personnel were often urgently needed to man newly built ships or ships which were under construction or being refitted, one way of ensuring this was the organisation of a quick disembarkation. Considerable difficulties were sometimes experienced in the stowage of the baggage on board, in order that the men might be disembarked in the minimum of time. It appeared that ratings on draft, as they were called, could proceed in two directions:

(i) to Asbury, for all ratings for the USA, Trinidad, Bermuda, South America and ships in the USA; and (ii) for Canada. As all ratings in (i) proceeded to Asbury, irrespective of their future movements, the draft would therefore leave the transport in two separate and distinct parties. It was therefore directed that depots and authorities should issue men with red and green labels. Red was for those proceeding to Asbury and green for those to Canada. These labels had to be pasted on the base of the kitbags and in a conspicuous place on the bunks.

Instructions had to be given to the Baggage Master of the ship to stow all the baggage with red labels on the port side of the hold and all those with green labels on the starboard side. By this arrangement, baggage could be disembarked according to the wishes of the immigration authorities as complete drafts. The immigration authorities in America had also stated that no officer or man could enter the United States unless he had been vaccinated and inoculated within the preceding twelve months. On investigation, on one voyage in May 1943, it was discovered that out of a total of 554 passengers, it was necessary to vaccinate 250 and inoculate 150. Apparently this caused a lot of trouble on board. The medical examinations for each rating on leaving their depot had not, in most cases, been carried out, resulting in a long and laborious procedure to discover the information on board!

It was a common occurence, too, for the *Queen Elizabeth* to carry a great many German POWs, bound for Canada. Normally the Germans caused little trouble, but there were always a few arrogant types amongst them. Some of the crew members were rather afraid of these, especially when they encountered them in the alleyways, despite the fact that these Germans were under guard. This German arrogance often led to speculation as to what would happen to the ship should one of the POWs revolt and succeed in grabbing a member of the crew, using him as a hostage. Certainly, such an incident would have resulted in a lot of Germans being killed!

The POWs got three meals a day. One of their own men was detailed to collect the food from the galley, bring it to the tables, and then they would help themselves to the food. They were also allowed to shower and it was usual for a few of them at a time to do this, under the guard of a British military policeman. After these daily routines, some of the POWs undertook small chores around the ship. Some would be taken up on deck and were ordered to sweep it, under the supervision of a crew member. On one of these occasions, the supervising quartermaster noticed one of the men limping slightly and asked him how he had been wounded. The German replied to the effect that he had been aboard a U-boat which had been captured by the British. All on board were ordered not to abandon the submarine until a lifeboat was sent across to them. He had ignored this order, and jumped into the sea, wherupon the destroyer opened fire on him. To this the quartermaster laughed and retorted

'Well, if you disobey orders, you have to accept the consequences'!

Other prisoners helped in the various kitchen departments, also under guard. The ship's crew got to know some of these quite well and would endearingly give them nicknames such as 'Eddy', 'Charlie,', 'Fritz,' etc. A few of these could speak quite good English. However, there were also others, some of whom had actually been educated in England, who could speak and understand English extremely well, which fact they kept strictly to themselves. The majority of them, however, were just ordinary men, who had been caught up in the horror of having to fight a war and had been captured whilst doing so, and they were quite happy to help out whenever asked. Some of them helped with the washing up and were more than happy when they were given ice cream and other titbits from the crew in return for their services.

On some occasions, the POWs were allowed to stage their own concerts in the mess hall. The crew were allowed to attend these entertainments and they also enjoyed these moments of hilarity even though, in the main, the proceedings were carried out in German. On one occasion they were entertained by two clowns, who had the reputation in pre-war days of being the best in their field in Europe. On another occasion one of the prisoners dressed himself up to represent General Montgomery. Two other men were disguised as a camel and 'General Montgomery' rode upon the back of this fictitious animal. The pantomime was so amusing on this occasion that both sides of the audience were in hysterics at the antics of 'General Montgomery', yelling instructions at his 'camel'.

Amongst these prisoners were also a number of very good artists, whose talents were also put to good use in helping paint the ship. There were always one or two of these men, who would try to be too artistic. Their guards found that if they turned their backs for a minute, in that brief space of time, a prisoner had painted swastikas everywhere. Others used to get hold of small, empty cartons, write all kinds of messages on these—'Q.E.iz.N.Atl.' and the like—and try to dump these over the side in the hope of their being picked up by a German ship. If this ruse had been successful, a German ship might soon have been on the scene with a bid to sink the *Queen Elizabeth*.

It was realised by the crew on board, however, that many of these Germans did not actually believe that they were sailing on board the *Queen Elizabeth*. Hitler's propaganda machine had, on different and several occasions, issued bulletins to the effect that both the *Queens* had been sunk by the 'illustrious German Navy'.

It was interesting for the crew to note, however, that whenever the lifeboat-drill alarm sounded, a number of the prisoners became quite hysterical, assuming that the ship was sinking and they were being left behind—which all went to show that even the bravest of men are human and show signs of fear on occasion.

One crew member recalls that on arriving in New York late one night, a British MP on duty came up to tell him that one of the German prisoners was feeling very ill, and could he come up on deck to get some air, because the stench below decks was absolutely appalling. The poor fellow was allowed to come up on deck, looking as if he were dying, accompanied by a German major, who was also a doctor. Whilst the sick man was gulping in the fresh air and thanking God for being allowed this period of relief, the German doctor stood looking at the blaze of lights that

signalled New York, New York—he was quite awestruck at the sight and cried out 'We're here . . we're here in New York!' The watchkeeper was by no means as impressed and called out to him 'Hey, Fritz . . . never mind bloody New York—just so you look after your sick friend here!'

Later in her Atlantic service after D-Day, the *Queen Elizabeth* carried an ever increasing number of sick and wounded, coming from the European battle zone. Sometimes up to 4,000 of these veterans were carried, some of whom were able to walk and sleep on the bunks. To cope with the men who needed more attention, the internal fittings of the ship were changed again and a great number of the Standees were removed before the commencement of the return voyage. Beds, stretchers, mattresses and pillows were provided and these were placed on top of the canvas backing of the Standees.

To cope with all these extra nursing duties, the permanent medical staff of doctors and nurses was

Wounded American soldiers rest on rafts on the deck (Imperial War Museum).

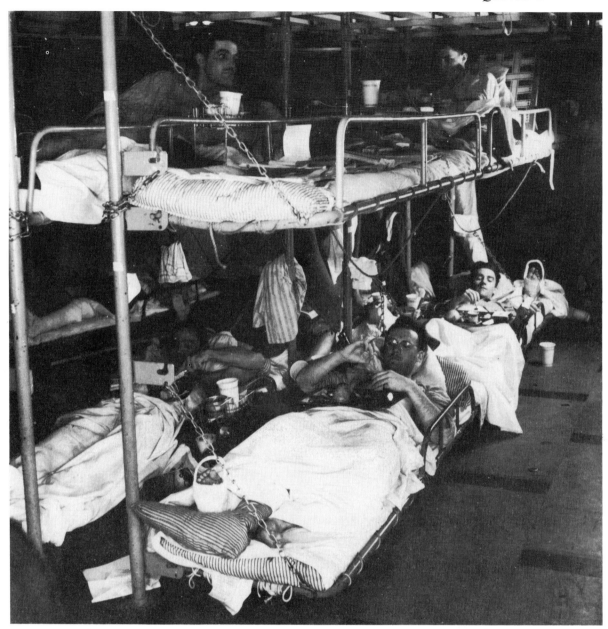

Hospitalised troops below decks on their way home (Imperial War Museum).

enlarged to 80, and, including the orderlies to assist them, the total medical staff sometimes totalled more than 400.

The nurses had initially travelled to England with the troops and had also disembarked at Gourock. In Europe they had been well trained to cope with nursing casualties, and they were now urgently needed on this return journey to nurse the hundreds of wounded who were being repatriated back to the States.

At the end of such a voyage, lines of ambulances would be waiting to take these casualties to Army base hospitals and, in a matter of only hours, the *Queen Elizabeth* would again have the feeling of being an empty ship. Not for long though—even in this short time, preparation for storing and refuelling were already under way, in readiness for the return voyage to England, within a couple of days, this time carrying a further 16,000 healthy troops as battle reinforcements.

Chapter 9

On the other side—the crew

Embarking, disembarking, feeding and accommodating these thousands of troops, without any delay or disturbance, planning the vessel to sail at appointed times and keeping her away from enemy attacks, was the tremendous task of the British Admiralty, the Ministry of War, the American Army's transport authorities and the Cunard officials, a task which they managed with sheer brilliance.

However, after returning from their briefing ashore and casting off, within the following two hours, the enormous job of getting the ship safely across an ocean alive with enemy vessels, without

the loss of one life, was in the hands of the Captain and his crew.

The responsibility for the ship and her live cargo rested entirely on the shoulders of the 'Old Man' and must have been very heavy indeed during the years of hostilities—at times insupportable.

He gained strength, however, from the knowledge that he was surrounded by more than capable officers and crew—some 1,000 contributing their services, many of them over a period of some years. A breakdown follows:

Staff Captain: was responsible for internal

An officer on watch on the bridge talks over the intercom (Imperial War Museum).

'The Old Man' (Captain Fall) giving his directions (Imperial War Museum).

A group of officers posing on the port wing. The four at the back are standing on the gyro-repeater platform, W.D. Heighway on extreme right. Front line, left to right: Bob Kissel, US Artillery Captain; R. Rhymes, Junior Second Officer; E. Irvine, Junior First Officer; Harold Baker, US Artillery Lieutenant; Cyril Calcutt, Senior Second Officer (Troop Officer); 'Butch' Bullen, RNVR Commander; Alan Henderson, Chief Officer (he should have an extra strip—3½ in all); A.H. Gill, Senior First Officer; others unknown.

organisation, with no navigational responsibilities. Deputy to the Captain.

Chief Officer: officer-in-command on the 4-8 Watch and responsible for the stability of the ship.

Senior First Officer: officer-in-command on the 12-4 Watch and assigned duties to deck crew.

Junior First Officer: officer-in-command on the 8-12 Watch and called the 'Navigator', as he was responsible for all the navigational equipment.

Senior Second Officer: called the 'Troop Officer', he had internal duties only, worked under the Staff Captain and dealt with any matter affecting the troops.

Junior Second Officer: Assistant Watch-Keeper on the 4–8 Watch, he assisted the Chief Officer in determining the ship's stability.

Third Officers, Senior, Intermediate and Junior: one assisted on the 8-12 Watch, one on the 12-4 Watch and one was the 'Night Officer', on duty internally from 9.00 pm to 6.00 am. These duties were rotated every week or voyage when on the North Atlantic run.

At least three times during the night hours, the Night Officer patrolled the ship with the senior master-at-arms on duty. This duty was carried out both in port and at sea and the Night Officer reported verbally to the Senior Officer-on-Watch on the bridge, after completing his rounds. A written report was then made to the Staff Captain. Responsibility for the internal safety and security of the ship was in the hands of ten masters-at-arms, policemen, watchmen and patrolmen stationed in various positions throughout the vessel. Time-clocks were also located throughout the ship and these had to be punched by the patrolling master-at-arms at specified times.

In theory, the Captain also inspected the ship each day about 10.00 am. However, as he rarely left the vicinity of the bridge whilst the ship was at sea, this duty was usually carried out by the Staff Captain.

Included in the deck department personnel were the radio officers and WRNS (cipher officer and coders). In the case of the WRNS, it was submitted that the policy of relieving a proportion of officers and ratings after only two round trips, was not in the best interests of the service, ship or personnel. Captain Fall, Master of the *Queen Elizabeth*, held very strong views on this matter and requested the OC Naval Personnel to report that, in his opinion, the practice did not make for smooth working and that it was unfair to the people concerned. (Their work was sufficiently arduous without imposing on them the task of constantly training newcomers).

On occasions, through sickness, two officers or two coders might be called on to work the watch. Under these circumstances, if one was untrained and hence not efficient (however zealous), her counterpart could not conscientiously hand over the watch to her. Likewise, if the novice did take over, could the Master have complete confidence in her? Further, it rather looked as though service in this particular ship was regarded by some volunteers as a holiday. To counteract this, it was submitted for consideration that (a) appointment of officers and the drafting of coders would be permanent and (b) that four officers and four coders were the complement of the *Queen* with

one officer and one coder 'standing off' for the duration of one round trip, though not necessarily being on leave throughout the whole of that period to which approval was given.

Ratings with bridge duties were: Six quartermasters, two per watch; three bridge messengers, one per watch; three Royal Navy signallers, one per watch; six look-outs, two per watch; and RN radar technicians, one or two per watch.

Quartermasters were responsible for steering the ship for two hours each watch and for the general bridge maintenance and stand-by duties. The bridge messengers were responsible for bridge cleaning and the messenger service, as well as answering the telephones. The RN signallers performed any visual signalling, when necessary. The RN radar technicians worked in the radar shack on the monkey island and they telephoned target information to the bridge.

When the ship was in range of enemy aircraft it was usual to have an officer or other rank, recruited from the troops aboard, to identify approaching aircraft, Look-outs worked in the crow's nest and on the monkey island. One look-out worked from monkey island and the

Port wing of the bridge—forenoon watch 8–12 am, North Atlantic, westbound towards New York on a fine, cold morning in 1943.

other went aloft into the crow's nest. In the case of the 12-4 Watch, the man on monkey island would be relieved by one of the watches on deck at 1.30 pm. He would then go below for a 30-minute coffee or smoke break. At 2.00 pm he relieved his colleague up in the crow's nest, where he would remain until 4.00 pm, completing his two-hour watch at this station. The look-out who had been relieved in the nest then had a 30-minute break, until 2.30 pm, when he relieved the man from the watch on deck (who had originally arrived on the bridge at 1.30 pm). It took five minutes to get from the monkey island to the mess room and then a few minutes getting aloft, up the steel ladder inside the mast to take over the watch in the crow's nest. In fine weather, with a fair wind, getting aloft those 107 steps proved no problem, and in this kind of weather the glass window was hinged up and hooked to the canopy of the crow's nest. In bad weather, however, it was an entirely different story—then it was a case of waiting until the ship lifted to the sea, then, almost weightlessly, running as far aloft as possible before the ship pitched. It was almost impossible to struggle against the force of gravity.

Up aloft, the canvas dodger was stuffed at the edges with old blankets and life-preservers in an effort to make the crow's nest snug in winter, and an electric heating unit was also installed to further this purpose. The dodger, hove to a jackstay on the canopy and the sides of the mast, was beautifully sewn by a Clyde sailmaker when the ship was initially rigged but later replaced by a green machine-sewn unit with punched eyelets of metal, in New York in 1944.

Later on in the war these lookouts were issued with binoculars, but the board also had a brass indicator for spotting the bearing of a ship or object in sight, which then had to be reported. This reporting was handled by a telephone. It was just a case of opening the 'phone-box, pressing a button and the answer from the bridge came through straight away, no receiver was required, simply a mouth piece and a speaker. This instrument was called the 'Loudaphone'.

Shortly after the cessation of hostilities the ship was making her way up the English Channel when the look-out 'phoned the bridge and was told that he had to keep a special watch for floating mines which had come adrift in the various fields. Later, while taking a sweep around with the glasses he saw, right ahead of the ship, one of these ugly, horned monsters. He 'phoned the bridge immediately, to be told that they had already picked this up on the radar and some of the officers had also picked it up through their glasses. This was quite a frightening situation because, as soon as the war ended, all her guns

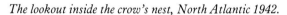

The lookout inside the crow's nest, North Atlantic 1942.

had been dismounted and the personnel on board had no way of exploding this floating mine. So, it had to be a case of good navigation, easing the ship over very slightly, so that the mine floated harmlessly down the port beam as they passed about 250 ft away!

Life up aloft in the crow's nest was, in some ways, a job to be enjoyed. The bosun's chair had been slung for comfort and someone had rigged up a foot rest for even more comfort! At least when one was on duty up there the air was clear and fresh and you were well away from the normal stench of the ship. It was also a thrill and most impressive to see the actual size of the vessel from that great height. Usually only the crew member on duty was allowed up in this vicinity, but on odd occasions a visitor—a soldier or another member of the crew—would be allowed up for a very short visit. There was not really enough room for two persons up there, hence the brevity of visits. The return to deck of these visitors always caused amusement. After clambering down the ladder and stepping through the hatch-door, two men would be there to pick them up; their exposure to the ship's movement at such a great height would have thrown their equilibrium completely out of balance. However, a few minutes lying on the deck soon brought them back to normal.

Sailors on watch did all the maintenance and overhauling of the ship's gear on deck, life-boats etc. There were four bosuns, three of them as watch-keepers on deck and one as the day bosun, each of whom had a gang of workers under his supervision.

There was never too much concern about smoke. Although this was usually kept to a minimum at sea it was never too minimal for the funnel not to need cleaning. As with any other ship, things still had to be repainted in order to keep the ship in good condition. Frequently she was painted by crew members who sat on the inboard gunwale of the life-boats, while the bosun's mate lowered the boat from the boat deck. This was quite a pleasant job compared with cleaning down the funnels, which were heavily blackened at the tops and after sides. This job was achieved from a bosun's chair, with a bucket of 'Sujee Mujee' attached. This meant climbing up inside the funnel and out through a small hatch, on to 'the deck', through which were outlets from the engine-room for smoke, on which the crew stood and rigged the chairs. This meant that the rim of the funnel was about chest high and thus cleaning them, as can be imagined, was a very, very filthy job. Its one consolation was the fact that as soon as the job was completed the crew cleaned up and had the rest of the day free. If

George Gilbertson, lookout, with his back to the warmth of the cabin.

Above *The lamptrimmer in the forepeak, Mr Allan E. Alday.* Queen Elizabeth *1943.*
Below *Spruced up and ready for action again. Note the white topmasts—even in wartime grey she looks graceful* (US National Archives).

they were in port, this meant that they could go straight ashore until the next morning.

However, painting the masts was the worst job and certainly the most dangerous. The man painting the top of the foremast was lowered by hand, with a couple of turns on the drum-end of the winch when slack was required. There was absolutely no margin for error, otherwise the bosun's chair at the end of the gant-line would come hurtling down from aloft with the man inside it. The topmasts were painted white in an endeavour to make them invisible against the skyline, not to minimise the size of the vessel, as some people thought.

The engine department comprised some 250 people of whom about one hundred were engineer officers, under the Chief Engineer and the Staff Chief Engineer. Throughout the war they had the enormous task of keeping the *Queen Elizabeth* going at high speeds and ensuring that all other services necessary for the ship to fulfil her task, worked in good order. Although very little is known of what actually happened down there in the bowels of this vessel, one might say that the feat of running these ship's engines, which had actually never been run in, through six very dangerous years without suffering any critical damage, will certainly not be surpassed.

The catering department, which included the Purser's office and department, consisted of some thirty people and was controlled by the Purser, the Chief Steward and the Second Steward. The complement also included chefs, cooks, butchers, bakers, pantrymen, confectioners, waiters, store-keepers, stewards and kitchen porters, as well as the printing shop.

There were some twenty butchers in the ship, assisted by the same number of troops, working in two shifts to prepare roughly 7,000 lbs of meat per day. To the personnel of the catering department it was considered an added bonus whenever the vessel ran into heavy weather for then most of the troops would be seasick and eating was the last thing they wanted to think about. The preparation and serving of the meals were the two main tasks undertaken by the catering department, though they were also responsible for the cleaning of the 'passenger departments' in the ship, in which task they were also assisted by troops.

The permanent staff was recruited from the various forces and all remained on the ship. They served as liaison between the crew and the troops, and included gunners, medical officers, security officers, nursing sisters, the Provost Marshal, intelligence officers, the Chaplain, the Paymaster,

An engineer on duty at the control panel of one of the main engines.

the baggage officer, Red Cross officials and orderlies, making a total of some 80 persons. A British Colonel was OIC Troops with a Major as his staff officer, and an American Colonel would act as second-in-command.

In general, they maintained good order and discipline in the ship and assisted in the embarkation, disembarkation, quartering and messing of the troops and at emergency drills. The permanent staff helped plan much of the detail for this, in conjunction with the officers of the various troops on board. Staff officers met with the Staff Captain each morning to be briefed accordingly.

On board the *Queen Elizabeth* there was also a permanent military medical staff comprising a Lieutenant-Colonel who was Senior Medical Officer, two medical officers, a surgical specialist, two nursing sisters, one warrant officer and some 28 others, serving as nursing orderlies and clerks, all from the Royal Army Medical Corps. Of course this complement was totally inadequate to care for the 15,000 troops on board and usually American officers, and as many nurses as could be

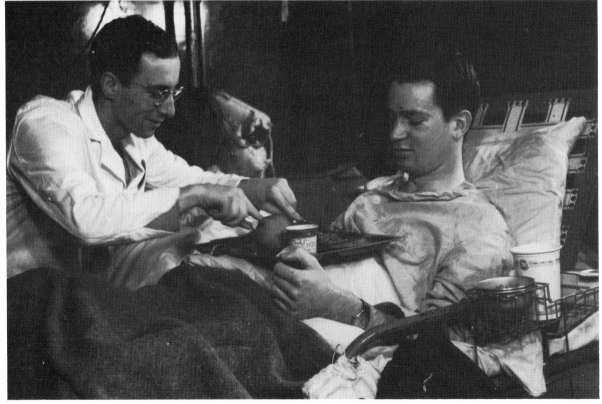

recruited from those on board, were assigned duties to help out the medical staff.

Sailing under such stressful conditions for so long caused tension in the ship. The crew signed six months' articles, but these could be extended to two years' if necessary. The crew suffered greatly from fatigue because, for many of them, the daily routine consisted of long, hard work, mainly in artificial light, for many, many hours. For some periods they did not see daylight for several days, unless they were working on deck. Each night the clocks would go forward one hour on the North Atlantic, which meant that one hour's additional sleep was lost as well. It was impossible to plead sickness as the attitude onboard was that 'If you can stand, you can walk and if you can walk, you can work. So there were NO sick people!'

No mail from home was received whilst on board and, in the case of Australians and others similarly far from home, up to nine months could elapse before they received letters from home.

Christmas and the New Year passed by like a normal Sunday, with no efforts made for extra celebrations, with the exception of the few gifts donated by people ashore for the crew, consisting of needles and thread, sweaters, scarves, knitted wool caps and sea-boot socks knitted in heavy, white wool, which were especially welcome. Religious life on board was practically non-existent, and the crew were not encouraged to attend any religious service.

To give some zest to life in this mundane existence, the crew had their own methods of making fun in the limited spare time they had between their watches. Every day at sea, between 4.00 pm and 6.00 pm, the troops officer, called 'the Procurer' by his fellow deck-officers, went out to 'procure' Nurses, WRNS, WAVES, WACS etc, for an afternoon tea party in the ward room. Tea would be served and there would be dancing. Alcohol was seldom found there and certainly not amongst the US troops on board but still, for the people who could attend these occasions, 'they had a great war'! The majority of the crew, however, were too tired to partake of

Above left *A staff meeting between service chiefs in 'the conference room'—a daily occurence at 10:00 hours* (Imperial War Museum).
Left *A medical orderly assists a wounded GI with his food* (Imperial War Museum).

Right *Certificate of sterling notes held by a seaman (Oswald Brett) and required by HM Customs boarding officer on return to a UK port.*
Next page *Seaman's formal certificate of discharge—this is one belonging to the artist, Oswald Brett.*

Identity card issued A.Y.A. 1218727   R.O. N/c   Dis. 1.

CERTIFICATE OF DISCHARGE

FOR A SEAMAN DISCHARGED BEFORE A SUPERINTENDENT OR A CONSULAR OFFICER

ISSUED BY THE
MINISTRY OF SHIPPING.   No. **26**   26/59   BADGE M.N ISSUED

Name of Ship and Official Number, Port of Registry and Gross Tonnage.	Horse Power.	Description of Voyage or Employment.	
"QUEEN ELIZABETH" 166290 LIVERPOOL 83673.02	158,000	**GOVERNMENT SERVICE**	

Name of Seaman.	Year of Birth.	Place of Birth.
O. BRETT	1921	Sydney

Rank or Rating.	No. of R.N.R. Commission or Certif.	No. of Cert. (if any).
SAILOR		

Date of Engagement.	Place of Engagement.	Copy of Report of Character.*	
		For Ability.	For General Conduct.
22 OCT 1941	SYDNEY.	VERY B 152 GOOD	VERY B 152 GOOD

Date of Discharge.	Place of Discharge.		
1 JUN 1942	GLASGOW		

I certify that the above particulars are correct and that the above named Seaman was discharged accordingly.

Dated this .... day of .... 19 ......   AUTHENTICATED BY

_____ MASTER.   _J. Kirkwood._
                                     Signature of Superintendent or Consular Officer.

* If the Seaman does not require a Certificate of his character, enter "Endorsement not required" in the spaces provided for the copy of the Report.

Signature of Seaman .... Oswald Brett. ....

NOTE.—Any person who forges or fraudulently alters any Certificate or Report, or copy of a Report, or who makes use of any Certificate or Report, or copy of a Report, which is forged or altered or does not belong to him, shall for each such offence be deemed guilty of a misdemeanour, and may be fined or imprisoned.

N.B.—Should this Certificate come into the possession of any person to whom it does not belong, it should be handed to the Superintendent of the nearest Mercantile Marine Office, or be transmitted to the Registrar-General of Shipping and Seamen, Tower Hill, London, E.C.3.

such merriment and in the main confined themselves to their quarters to sleep, read, chat and sometimes to invite one of the troops to come into their quarters. Diaries, cameras and drawing material were strictly forbidden and if a diary should be found this was immediately censored. However, amongst 16,000 troops or even only 2,000 this ruling was difficult to enforce.

Even though no printed regulations were actually issued concerning people drawing or sketching whilst at sea, it was known that this was considered an illegal pastime. It did occur, however, and it was a case of the 'artist' keeping a low profile and making a sketch from a porthole or wherever he could. Generally, the authorities turned a blind eye and, in the case of the artist who contributed towards this history, it was well known on board that he was making such illustrations. Several people asked him to sketch or make a painting of the ship and, indeed, one of his drawings was presented to Captain Fall by the officers, on the occasion of his wedding in 1944.

Right *Walter Clarke, AB,* Queen Elizabeth *1943.*
Below *The painting presented to Captain Fall on the occasion of his wedding January 11 1944. The work was carried out by Oswald Brett AB, later to become known for his maritime studies in oil. The card was printed on board in the* Queen Elizabeth's *printing shop.*

PRESENTED TO

CAPTAIN E. M. FALL. C.B.E., D.S.C., R.D., R.N.R.

H.M.T. "QUEEN ELIZABETH"

By his Staff Captain, Navigating and Gunnery Officers,
on the occasion of his wedding, 11th January, 1944

A formal group of the Queen Elizabeth's *staff officers on the sun deck* (Imperial War Museum).

The card was printed in the printing shop and inset into the mount surrounding the drawing. On another occasion the artist was asked by the Captain to paint the name on one of the ship's life-preservers, to use it as a frame for a picture! Occasionally he would be called up to the 'Old Man's' stateroom, to letter his name and address on his crates, being sent ashore with food stuffs or other items the latter had purchased in the USA.

The Captain had his suite on the starboard side of the ship and this seemed a world remote and luxurious from that of the crew quarters. Honey-coloured, polished wood panelling, a telephone with a white handset and a heavy curtain hanging in the open doorway was enough to inspire awe and a great sense of authority and command—which even on social occasions was an overpowering experience.

All the crew accommodation was the same as in peace-time. The Senior Third Officer's cabin, for example, was on the port side, below the bridge and was 'L' shaped. It was sited in the officers' accommodation area and one deck below the

Captain's cabin. Navigation and radio officers had their own two ward rooms and WRNS were accommodated in cabins on the boat deck, which had originally been constructed as staterooms. deck officers, radio officers and WRNS dined in the tourist dining room, along with commissioned officers of the Forces on board and were served by stewards. Sittings were in two sessions and three meals a day were served. Engineers, however, had their own accommodation and mess-room on the sun deck.

Sailors and kitchen personnel etc, were all accommodated below. Some shared a two-berth cabin whilst others slept eight to a cabin. Sleep, especially for the ones sleeping in the bows, was frequently difficult. When the vessel pitched in heavy seas, the anchor chain in the hawse would make a terrible noise every time she went up or down, which would then vibrate into the crew's quarters.

Some of the crew furnished their quarters with all kinds of 'loot' in the way of chests, rugs etc, which had been sited in the passenger

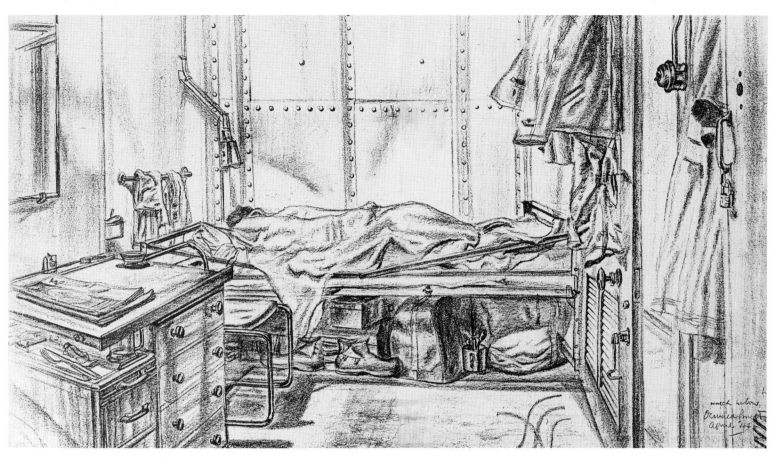

Above *Oswald Brett's shipmate Bob Thompson—watch below—asleep in his berth. Oswald's bunk is against the ship's side (he drew it from there). Note the sheer of the ship with deck sloping aft (to right). Rug, chair, mirror and little chests under table top have been 'acquired' from the passenger accommodation. Steel lockers for clothing are at right, door ajar.*

Right *Oswald Brett and his shipmate Walter 'Nobby' Clark pose for an informal picture on the foredeck of the* Queen Elizabeth.

accommodation earlier in the war. Chairs and mirrors had also been earmarked, but, much to their chagrin, these were later taken away by the Chief Officer, when all remaining furniture was brought ashore in New York. Some enterprising crew members still managed to find some surplus furnishings but, in the main, the accommodation was quite spartan. The berths had all been made of wood when war broke out, but had been replaced by steel-framed cots in New York early in 1943. At the same time bunk lights had been fitted. (Individual berth lights had not been available for the crew before the war.) The only privacy available in such conditions was that

The crowd—crew mess room—North Atlantic, March 1945. Note wood 'fiddles' on the bulkhead for putting on the tables in bad weather to keep bottles and plates in place.

improvised by oneself, for example by hanging a towel as a curtain on a line besides or above the bunk or strung from whatever else was handy.

The sense of good fellowship and friendliness in such crowded living conditions was about the only thing that redeemed such a life. Although very crowded and generally considered awful, the condition were still a vast improvement on the 'sailing-ship' style which still existed in many other ships and the *Queen Elizabeth* was very clean. A typical example of sailors' conditions was the sailors' mess-room (R deck, forward). This was furnished with quite good chairs and presentable tables covered in washable formica. This compared well to most other ships, which sported mess-rooms with scrubbed wooden tables and forms or benches that also had to be scrubbed down.

The food served to them was good. It was brought to them by mess-men, the Sailor's Peggy' from the galley, carried in enamelled kits

in tiers of two or three, covered by tea-towels, which one could hold by the corners. These were then placed on hot stainless steel tops, by the sink, so that food was kept warm. The crew would come and pick a plate out of a rack, which had been designed so as to prevent crockery moving around in bad weather. Each man went along, put his own meat and vegetables on the plate and carried it back to a place at one of the tables. There were about eight tables, each capable of seating six men. All condiments were kept permanently on the tables. When the main course was finished, the plate was taken back into the scullery where the mess-men would wash the dishes. Dessert came in the form of coffee, pudding, stewed or canned peaches or fruit salad. On Sundays, ice cream would also be served and half a roast chicken would be added to the main course.

Fresh fruit was also supplied, the mess-man

bringing this around to the crew. The crew each carried his own mug, knife, fork and spoon which could be left either in their cabin or in the mess-room. The mug was also utilized for holding a pint of beer in the crew's bar, the *'Pig and Whistle'*, where cigarettes also could be purchased. Items such as bars of chocolate, crackers or soft drinks could be obtained in the troops' canteen. Ground coffee, hot water, condensed milk, salads and cakes were also left out on a little table outside the scullery, so that anyone could help himself if he felt like extra sustenance. Clean linen was supplied to all the sailors once a week and the 'Sailor's Peggy' would go around to pick up all the dirty linen. Despite the luxuries they were supplied in the way of food, compared with the majority of the people in Europe, the biggest treat those crew members looked forward to, was their shore leave.

Whilst Cunard appreciated the need for shore leave for the crew to maintain contact with families and to give the men a chance to get away from it all, it was impossible to send all crew members home at once. The company therefore devised a scheme whereby at the end of each returning voyage to a British port, part of the crew were sent home for one round voyage, another portion rotated in having 48 hours' local leave to visit family, friends or to attend to personal affairs, and the rest of the crew remained on board. Those leaving the ship were brought ashore in the same tenders that carried the troops to Gourock. On the return journey, the tenders brought back temporary workers to the vessel. The crew were all issued with return rail tickets and vouchers to any destination in the UK. At this stage, the crew comprised a variety of nationalities. In August 1942, some of the Australian members of the crew, who had come to England after that long voyage to the Middle East, wanted to leave the ship and return home as soon as was possible. Half of these were allowed to leave and the majority of them were put aboard the *Ceramic* for this return voyage. Unfortunately,

Shipmates ashore! Four crew members pose for a London photographer. Left to right: Alfred Wakenshaw, Syd Fallowfield, George King and Bill Morgan.

this vessel was torpedoed off the Azores on December 6 and all ex-crew members, with the exception of one, were lost. The news of this terrible loss caused great shock and sadness amongst the crew members still aboard the *Queen Elizabeth*.

Dry-docking was also a time to look forward to. A good place, albeit rather spartan, was Bayonne, New Jersey, which was then a military dry dock. Late in January 1943, the *Queen Elizabeth* was to follow the Vichy French ship *Richelieu* into this dry dock. At the time westerly gales were sweeping across, heavy snow had fallen and it was freezing cold, and because of these conditions, entrance to the dry dock was delayed for a few days. The Captain then decided they could delay no longer, so he took a gamble and decided to take the ship in. Unfortunately, as the vessel was sliding into the dry dock, the wind changed and, despite the efforts of the tugs to assist her, she hit the side of the dock, damaging some portholes. Rumour had it that there was thick weed beneath her, which would bring her to a standstill. This proved untrue but, as usual, rumours like this got around frequently and, in the 'getting' grew every time!

The dry dock was under the strict guard of formidably armed US marines, who used to travel around the dock in jeeps, wearing fur caps and looking for trouble. Ship's personnel were strictly confined to the vessel. The Chief Engineer was held up on one occasion by the marines, who thought him a saboteur! If you did manage to get shore leave, you were driven by bus out of the dry dock and then transferred onto another bus, going to Jersey City, from where you could get the subway system right into Manhattan. The facilities in the dry dock left much to be desired. As the ship was shut down, toilets, washing and showering had to be done ashore in a big shed close to the gangway. Later the crew could remain on board although there were still restrictions on the use of toilets, showers etc, as the discharge was led away from the ship's side by a special hose-fitting shored against an opening in the side. When the ship was fumigated the crew were taken ashore and housed in various hotels for one night of luxury! All external openings were closed and warning signs were displayed, whilst drawers and cupboards were to be open. Fumigators often used cyanide which could be thrown into the corners as well. After being sealed for about four

Seaman's Mission and the old Staten Island ferry building. This is the street bordering the East River, north from the Battery.

hours the ship was again opened up by the fumigators wearing masks. Forced ventilation started as soon as possible (ASAP in the crew's jargon). Large ships such as the *Queen Elizabeth* could be fumigated in sections and other parts of the ship could remain fully operative when necessary. If the ship was shut down completely a major hazard could occur should anything go wrong! When fumigation was completed and the ship declared 'free' again, life on board returned to normal with all its inconveniences!

The most favoured place of all, however, was the pier at West 50th Street in Manhattan—that was something everyone agreed on. Located midtown, it was a matter of only a few minutes' walk or a couple of minutes' ride on the bus and you were right in the heart of New York. The sight of the Manhattan skyline was one that crews yearned for—it was the world's most desired port during the war and a place where you could literally buy anything.

Despite the 'glamour' of New York night-life, one of the havens for British seamen, during the war, was the Seamen's Church Institute and many of the crew on the *Queen Elizabeth* still have happy memories of the hours spent there. Whilst entertainment and recreational facilities in New York were expensive there was still plenty of amusement to be obtained cheaply or even for free.

The Australian crew members loved New York; for some of them it was their first experience of snow and ice, and some amusing episodes are recalled due to these conditions. On one occasion it became apparent that meat scraps were being dumped over the side of the ship but the butchers involved had not realised that the harbour was partly frozen over. This was noticed by a patrolling watchman, who came on board to investigate the incident. He found the instigator of the trouble to be an Australian butcher and promptly ordered that the latter be lowered over the side of the ship by rope and made to pick up the pieces of scrap and stow it in various bags! On another occasion, Australians in one of the ship's life boats during life-boat drill on the Hudson River, continued sailing right across to New Jersey. They beached the boat there, then took a taxi back to the ship, where a very irate Purser had to settle the account. Unfortunately, no record is available as to the sentence imposed upon these culprits.

Payment on the ship went far beyond the average need but many on board still went into a little business on the side. One AB, for instance, received about £24 per month, which he

subsided by the taking of anchor-watches whilst in New York or on the Clyde when the ship was in port on a Sunday. Incidentally, no overtime was paid for Sundays at sea. As it was only possible to draw a limited number of dollars on the ship in New York, on the way back to the UK, the crew would draw all their allotment in sterling and then exchange this with the US troops at $4.03 to the pound. Initially, the Americans would be reluctant to part with their money but, as the *Queen Elizabeth* got closer to the Clyde, they were just as anxious to exchange their money, as the crew were to buy it. It was possible to buy dollars ashore in New York but at the official rate they only received $2.80 to the pound.

As can be imagined, quite a lot of wheeling and dealing went on throughout the war on this run. Profiteering from the kitchen went on for the whole trip. The cooks fixed American-style hamburgers etc, and sold them to the GIs for up to 25c—a considerable sum when the GIs were paid only $21.00 per month. There was a critical lack of commodities and food in the UK that were still available in the States. The most common items were nylon stockings, cigarettes, meat, birdseed, watches and fountain pens. But carpets and dresses and other items of clothing were also amongst the articles brought back by crew members and taken through HM Customs without declaration. Some of the troops also played a part in this smuggling, by filling their life jackets with nylon stockings, and even throwing some of these overboard 'accidentally'. Ultimately, though, the crew were the real masters of the smuggling game.

On several occasions, troops noticed that the promised feast for Thanksgiving Day did not materialise. Later they saw crew members taking this food ashore at Gourock. Until then they had never realised how acute was the food shortage in Britain. The black market flourished on what was 'imported' from the USA via the various ships on the North Atlantic run!

The crew used all sections of the ship to stow away contraband and if the item were too big to be carried ashore unobtrusively through Customs, they used various crates in which spares were to be collected. One of the most fascinating hiding places was in the counterweights in the lift. The loot would actually follow the Customs officers up and was then removed and stowed away in another safe hiding place. Wood panelling was also removed, and the loot stowed in artificial cupboards between the ship's hull and the inner wall.

Once the goods were safely smuggled ashore,

they were directed to various railway stations throughout England, such as Liverpool and London, and then placed in the left-luggage offices there. Money would be exchanged when the ticket for the luggage was actually handed over to the receiver. He was the one then who went to redeem the luggage from the station.

This was a massive operation and things often went drastically wrong. One suitcase full of perishable items went astray in London. Rather than create a fuss about this, the receiver let it go. A few days later the suitcase started to smell and it was sent over to Scotland Yard. There it was identified, both by content and origin. Meanwhile the crew concerned in Scotland had been alerted as to this mishap and attempts had to be made to put all documentation in order to make this look as if it were a legitimate consignment!

Along the way, the American MPs who were posted on the ship's permanent staff decided to go into business with the crew and, from then on, goods were often stowed in US Mail bags.

It was the practice that, when the ship was berthed in Scotland, the Americans took over guard duty from the British, who were then allowed to go home for a couple of days leave. However, when 'Stateside', the reverse situation pertained and, in this way, everything could be brought on board quite safely. When the ship was in Gourock, the Americans would help the crew to unload the mailbags from the ship and, when asked by the Officer-in-Charge of Mailbags what

Coming up the Hudson River with the tugs joining her for the run up to Pier 90, 1944.

was in the bags, the Americans would simply call out 'Oh . . . US Mail and in those days the US Mail was sacrosanct!

Crew and guards got on very well with each other in this way and help from various people ashore was also offered, on the basis of 'if you scratch my back, I'll scratch yours'! It is as well to remember, though, that the goods being imported in this way were in no way connected with any illegal commodities such as drugs. They consisted of basic commodities, with the odd luxury item included, which helped to alleviate some of the gloom and shortages which existed in the UK. The seller, though, could make as much as 100 per cent profit on some items.

The old Scottish adage, quoted by Burns, 'The best laid plans of mice and men oft gang agley', was often brought to mind if a convoy had arrived there a few days ahead of the *Queen*. The crews aboard these ships were also engaged in the smuggling game and by the time the *Queen* arrived, the whole area was saturated with cigarettes and other commodities from the States. From the amount of smuggling which went on, the impression is that the security in these areas was very lax. This, however, was not the case. Security at British Customs was extremely tight and one had to have an inside contact before one could smuggle ashore an item the size of a carpet or the like. Security in New York was equally tight and, in some cases there, Customs and even MPs could confiscate goods which had actually been purchased on board the ship and, here again, one needed to know an 'inside' person.

Unauthorised persons were not allowed in the vicinity of the pier in New York. Crew members, on arrival there, had to surrender their British identity cards. They were issued with Alien Registration Certificates in 1943 when the US Immigration Authorities no longer treated the ship as a naval auxiliary, but as a passenger liner instead.

As always, people were able to find loopholes in the system and, despite tight security, there was also a small traffic in stowaways, using crew passes to come on board. Normally, a ship's crew member, who was acquainted with the plan, would stand at the ship's doorway to avoid any trouble. Probably the most interesting stowaway was a Canadian paratroop company's dog, who crossed the Atlantic once, together with his master.

Once the advance party came on board, all shore leave would be cancelled. For many of the crew this meant that contact with their friends and in many cases, their girl-friends, became impossible. Through the telephone exchanges people ashore would still try to contact them and quite often these calls were allowed, provided that no mention was made of the ship's ultimate destination. Despite this secrecy, people on board knew well in advance of sailing time what her destination was, but they did not know the actual route she would take. As always, the 'galley radio' would have many rumours flying around as to where she was going and how she would get there.

Some sixteen days further on, however, the people 'in the know' in New York would start looking out of their office windows with eagerness, their ears on the alert for that mighty sounding horn, which would shake the floors of the skyscrapers with her sonorous tones. Very slowly and majestically they would see her two huge funnels glide by—very shortly they could expect 'phone calls again from their boy-friends aboard the *Queen Elizabeth*.

Chapter 10

Former glory restored

The *Queen Elizabeth* commenced her last wartime Atlantic voyage on April 7 1945, when she carried more than 3,000 wounded soldiers to New York. On arrival there, she found her sister ship the *Queen Mary* already berthed and both ships stayed in port until after VE-Day.

The war at an end, the *Queen Elizabeth* started the job of repatriating American and Canadian troops back to their homelands. Gone were the blackouts, the zig-zagging, the fear of U-boat attacks or air harassment. Portholes could be left open throughout the day and night and the crew could finally take a breath of air.

At one point it had looked as if the mighty *Queen* was going to be required to carry American forces to the Pacific Theatre for the final assault against Japan. However, the dropping of the atomic bombs brought about a quick Japanese surrender and so the plan was shelved.

After VE-Day the armament was stripped from

Left *A cable informed the ship's personnel of President Roosevelt's death. The Red Duster is at half-mast, April 12 1945* (Imperial War Museum).
Below *Postcard which became available on board after the war had ended.*

The Cunard White Star Superliner "QUEEN ELIZABETH"
(On War Service)

Above *Off Gourock in better days in the summer of '45.*
Right *In this striking photograph taken from a US Coast Guard aircraft, cheering veterans are shown aboard the* Queen Elizabeth *as she approaches New York Harbor, June 29 1945* (US National Archives).

the ship in New York (Oerlikons, Bofors, rockets etc,)—only the heavier 3-in AA guns fore and aft, and the 6-in stern-chaser were taken ashore in Gourock later that summer.

She left New York again on June 14 to pick up her first load of returning Americans. Some 15,000 soldiers, sailors, nurses and civilians boarded the vessel in Gourock, to leave England on June 24. The imminent arrival of the *Queen Elizabeth* in New York had been heralded in all the newspapers and over the radio, so that when she approached the coast off Sandy Hook, blimps were hovering in welcome, playing music; sometimes their crews addressed the ship and her troops by asking questions—receiving stirring answers from the many thousands who were lining the decks. Gaily dressed, she steamed up

the Hudson to the warm welcome waiting her from the hundreds of ships and pleasure boats along the way. On one ship were Red Cross girls and WACs—and, at this point, a distinct list suddenly became noticeable on board the liner!

Flags were flown from apartment houses and from the windows of the New York skyscrapers. Ships in the harbour were bedecked cheerfully and scores of harbour craft were flying flags. Bands were playing welcoming music and, on the shore, crowds were waving madly, as a paper blizzard of ticker-tape and coloured paper showered down from the skyscrapers. It was as if the whole of New York had come out to welcome the return of the *Queen Elizabeth*. Every ship in the Hudson started to sound three long blasts, which were answered by the liner's deep tones as she

slowly nosed her way up to Pier 90. The cheering crowds, the bands, and the ships' sirens seemed unending and this tumultuous welcome brought a lump into the throat of many of the troops surveying this scene from the decks above.

Turnarounds, on both sides of the Atlantic were handled very quickly, for the troops wanted to get

back home as fast as possible. On her second voyage she brought back the 44th Division, who

Above *Returning troops get their first glimpse of the 'Big Apple' after a long time away* (Imperial War Museum).
Right *Almost alongside Pier 90, excited troops threaten to overturn the vessel* (Stewart Bale).

received the same ecstatic welcome. However, when coming round the pier they were confronted by a massive statue of Marlene Dietrich—the mascot of the 44th. The next return trip to Gourock was to be the last to her wartime base for, after so many loyal years, Gourock had to step down in favour of Southampton. Southampton was now ready to take on the task of embarking troops for their return to the States and the tenders, which had performed so proficiently in Gourock, were now no longer needed. On August 7 she sailed from Tail-of-the-Bank for the last time, her halyard flying the sign 'Thank You,' whilst the crew brought out a big, white sheet on which was painted 'Thank you, Gourock!' It was their own salute to Gourock, a place which had showered hospitality on the *Queen Elizabeth* through many exciting, dangerous hours and which for many troops had been their first glimpse of Europe. On the tender *King Edward* a pipe-band played music whilst Americans hung out of many of the portholes or lined the rails, showering candy, coins and cigarettes onto the band. What a scene—and what a contrast to her arrival there after her secret dash across the Atlantic five years before.

It was on August 20 1945, that the liner entered Southampton Docks for the first time. It was a drizzly, wet morning but still many people came out to watch the entry of 'Southampton's Baby'. In his welcoming address to the Mayor of Southampton, Captain Fall said that he was proud to be in command of such a great ship. He knew that Southampton had suffered many severe air raids and felt that he had been fortunate to have been away from this horror at sea, especially in a vessel like the *Queen Elizabeth*.

Seven days later she left the Solent, this time crowded with 15,000 United States Air Force personnel among whom was Colonel James Stewart, the film actor. As the vessel was swinging out, eight Meteor jets of the Royal Air Force flew in formation overhead, to salute their American colleagues.

Left *US troops, so glad to be home!*
Below *The last load of US troops embarking at Gourock, August 6–7 1945* (Imperial War Museum).

Between this time and October 1945, the *Queen Elizabeth* made three further voyages ferrying American personnel back home. On one of these trips, the trip from September 14 to 19 Commodore Sir James Bisset ordered that her funnels be repainted in Cunard Red and Black, although her hull still retained the battleship grey.

On her arrival in New York on October 9, the US officers of the permanent staff left their duties aboard the ship for the last time. In August, Prime Minister Attlee had asked President Truman for the 'return' of the ship, as Commonwealth servicemen also needed ferrying back to their homelands. After a few weeks of discussion it was decided that the *Queen Elizabeth*, together with the *Aquitania*, would be used for the carriage of Commonwealth troops to Canada, whilst the *Queen Mary* would continue the ferrying of Americans back to New York. On October 22 1945, with Canadian officers already attached to the permanent staff, the *Queen Elizabeth* commenced her task of repatriating an initial contingent of over 12,000 Canadian troops.

Halifax, Nova Scotia, was preferred by the Canadian government as the first port of call—for patriotic reasons they wanted their troops to set foot first on Canadian soil. However, Sir James Bisset, her new captain, would not even think of this for with winter fast approaching he considered Halifax to be a most dangerous and unsuitable spot for a ship like the *Queen Elizabeth*, taking into consideration the prime concern—the safety of the troops and the ship's crew. Also, Halifax had no enclosed dock and the quay used was really only a wharf, open to swell from the south-east. Thus a severe south-easterly gale could possibly break the ship from her moorings. Sir James was adamant on this matter and he had

Above left *The Anchorage at Gourock, Scotland on a fine August day in 1945.*
Below left *August 20 1945, dressed overall the* Queen Elizabeth *sails into Southampton for the first time* (Imperial War Museum).
Below *As the* Queen Elizabeth *leaves Southampton with US troops on August 27 1945, RAF Meteor jets bid them farewell* (Imperial War Museum).

the full backing of his fellow captains. They all thought it would be far wiser to disembark the troops in New York or Boston during the winter months and transport them from there by train to Canada.

The Canadian government immediately overruled these claims and said Sir James' fears were groundless. The Canadian Defence Minister, however, thought that the Canadian government should accept the Captain's decision since he was the Master of the ship, responsible for her safety, and therefore his decision should prevail.

Following the disagreement, an article appeared in the *Sunday Express* pointing out that sending the liner to New York just did not make sense. Difficulties were there to be overcome and the British people were sick and tired of being pushed into second place. No doubt the editor of that newspaper had never gone through the traumas of trooping in dangerous areas, otherwise he would have sided 100 per cent with the views of Sir James and his colleagues. However, Lord Beaverbrook, the owner of the newspaper, was extremely influential (and Canadian too) and the final decision was for Halifax to be the first Canadian port of call. On her arrival in Halifax on October 20 thousands of people had turned out despite the drizzling rain and gave a warm, cheering, rousing welcome to their compatriots.

Once back in Southampton again she needed dry-docking for a routine overhaul, before returning to Halifax with her second contingent of troops. From then on until March 6 1946, she made 12 Atlantic crossings, all to New York, either with US or Canadian troops. Winter conditions on the Atlantic were so bad that Halifax was regarded as incapable of giving protective shelter. On one of these trips she suffered from south-westerly gales with mountainous seas and on arrival in New York was caught in a tremendous blizzard. On this occasion the Canadians were transferred to special trains which were waiting for them on the harbour-side.

Usually a few civilians also made the Westbound voyage on board the *Queen Elizabeth*, most of them going to the US for business purposes. The most important of these passengers boarded the ship with his wife on January 9 1946, along with 12,000 returning Canadian personnel. Ex-Prime Minister Sir Winston Churchill,

smoking his now-famous cigar and his wife were en route to Florida for a well earned holiday. Every morning Sir Winston visited the bridge and monkey island. He had little conversation to offer but seemed content just to stand and stare at the waves through which the *Queen Elizabeth* ploughed. He and his wife were allotted a suite on the sun deck and more than enjoyed this, their first experience of being on board the liner. One day, prior to the ship's arrival in New York, Sir Winston was invited to address the troops and gave the following speech: 'My friends and shipmates on the *Queen Elizabeth*, for most of you it is homeward bound. It has been a good voyage, in a great ship with a fine Captain, or indeed, Commodore. We have not got there yet, but I am quite sure he will find the way all right. At any rate, he has been over the track before and, as I can testify myself having been several times with him in those days when there used to be U-boats and things like that. They all seem to have dropped off now, and we don't have to worry about them at all. Something has happened. The seas are clear, the old flag still flies and those who have done the work, (or some of it because the British did some before) return home again, their task accomplished, their duty done. Yesterday I was on the bridge, watching the mountainous waves and this ship, which is no pup, cutting through them and mocking their anger. I asked myself, why is it that the ship beats the waves, when they are so many and the ship is one? The reason is that the ship has a purpose and the waves have none! They just flop around, innumerable, tireless, but ineffective. The ship with the purpose takes us where we want to go. Let us, therefore, have purpose both in our national and Imperial policy, and in our own private lives. Thus the future will be fruitful for each and all, and the reward of the warriors will not be unworthy of the deeds they have done.'

On the eastbound trip, the *Queen Elizabeth* carried a great variety of people, the number of whom did not usually exceed 2,000. The majority was comprised of ATS (Auxiliary Territorial Service), WRNS, Polish Airmen and British POWs, all of whom were returning from the war in the Far East having landed in Canada and then been conveyed by train across to Halifax. There were also men from all British services, diplomats, Congressmen etc. Amongst these were numbered Mr Byrnes, US Secretary of

Left *Canadian Military personnel pass time on the sun deck on the first repatriation trip to Canada, October 22 1945. Note the Cunard colours and the Cunard White Star house-flag* (Public Archives, Canada, PS 113768).

State, the Canadian Prime Minister and his wife and Mrs Eleanor Roosevelt, who were all en route to a UNO Conference being held in London. Official members of their staffs also travelled on the liner, together with officials of the United Nations Relief and Rehabilitation Administration Organisation (UNRRA) who were bound for Europe to carry on their work among the refugees.

Civilians had their accommodation on a reserved part of A-deck, where they were allowed the use of a number of staterooms, a lounge and a small dining room.

A remarkable 'passenger' on one of these eastbound trips was a very valuable piece of cargo. It did not need a stateroom or even a bunk, for it travelled in a tin box. It was the 'Lincoln' copy of the Magna Carta, one of only four surviving copies of this ancient document, which had originally been preserved in Lincoln Cathedral, and had been sent on loan via the *Queen Mary* to

New York, for the World Fair in August 1939, where it had been retained for safekeeping at the outbreak of war. Initially, it had been placed in the Library of Congress in Washington, but, following the attack on Pearl Harbor, it was transferred for safer keeping to Fort Knox.

Trying to put this tin box in a safe place on board, posed quite a few problems as it was too big to go into the ship's safe. After much conjecture Sir James decided that the box be placed under his bed which he felt was probably the safest place on the ship. When this became public knowledge, great amusement was caused on board when the British press headlined their editions: 'Commodore sleeps with Magna Carta under his bed. First man in history to do so!'

On March 6 1946, the *Queen Elizabeth* entered the New Dock of Southampton at Berth 101, at the finish of her last voyage as a troop transport under wartime conditions, disembarking the last 1,709 out of the almost 750,000 passengers

Anchored off Gourock, spring 1946, work well under way in restoring the Queen Elizabeth *into what she was originally intended to be: the world's largest passenger liner* (The Times).

she had carried in the last six years. Having steamed more than 500,000 miles, she was now to be refitted and turned into the luxury liner she was originally meant to be. Temporary toilets, bulkheads, store-rooms, wash-places and all other troop fittings were taken out and put ashore. She had already been stripped of nearly 10,000 Standees and her life-jackets in New York. Many miles of wiring had to be dismantled and much of the furniture needed renewing or renovating.

Half her crew were paid off, some of them to take a long and well-deserved holiday, others to join new ships, while a skeleton crew of some 350 remained on board. They were needed for maintenance in port and to move her back up to the Clyde, where as much work as possible would be done before her return to the Southampton dry dock again. At this point she was nearly destroyed when fire broke out in the temporary isolation hospital on the promenade deck. Since this room had not been used as such for some time it had

become a store-room for drugs. Apparently one of these bottles had been broken, filling the room with fumes and so, when one of the workmen lit a cigarette in this isolated area, the whole ship was set on fire. Fortunately, after a three-hour struggle, the fire was under control and finally extinguished, although not before the deck was pushed up into a huge blister.

The renovations on the *Queen Elizabeth* began on March 31, after Sir James had anchored her off Gourock. For two and a half months John Brown's technicians, craftsmen and a variety of other workmen swarmed over the ship. The heavy degaussing cables were removed and hundreds of painters chipped off her wartime grey down to the waterline, applying an anti-corrosive paint coat and finally her Cunard livery—black hull, white superstructure and red funnels with black top and two thin, black rings.

Engineers overhauled all the ship's machinery and replaced working parts where necessary. Electricians checked all the wiring and electrical

A broadside view showing the difference in livery (The Times).

equipment, including lighting, intercoms, winches and kitchen equipment and also renewed parts which needed to be refitted. Plumbers, carpenters, joiners, furnishers and interior decorators were all responsible for the renewing and refurbishing necessary to return the ship to her former glory—it was as if she were reborn again.

Early in June, most of this heavy work was nearing completion, so the ship was taken down

Speed trials in the Firth of Clyde on October 8 1946 prior to entering service as a passenger liner (The Bulletin).

to Southampton to be dry-docked for overhaul of her rudder, propellers and for bottom painting. Here her interior fittings would be completed, using as many as possible of the original furnishings, which had been removed and stored in Singapore and Sydney.

Since the *Queen Mary* was still in her wartime grey and only slightly modified, the *Queen Elizabeth* became the first big British ship to be reconditioned, a lesson to the world that Britain was not sitting down to mourn her losses in the ashes of post-war desolation but that she was determined to rise again.

The *Queen Elizabeth* now became a

'wonder' ship and had everything she needed. No more Standee bunks crowded her public rooms for these had been lovingly restored and were beautifully panelled, decorated, fitted and furnished. She offered her passengers the ultimate in comfort and was now a floating city with drawing rooms, lounges, restaurants, writing rooms, smoking rooms, cinemas, shops, winter gardens, a library and many other facilities. Also she would carry no more than 2,260 passengers— 790 in first class, 680 in cabin class and 790 in the tourist class, and for all these people a seat was available in one of her 26 lifeboats.

On October 5 she was fitted out to the last detail and ready for her trials in the Firth of Clyde. She arrived early on the morning of October 7, and many VIPs came on board to have a look around her and to spend the night. Everything was ready for the official trials the next day.

At precisely 11.00 am the Royal party boarded the liner—Queen Elizabeth, her daughters, HRH Princess Elizabeth and HRH Princess Margaret, accompanied by their Ladies-in-Waiting and other personnel. They were introduced to the ship's officers and were escorted up to the bridge at 2.50 pm.

At that moment the vessel was turning into position for the first (northward) run over the

measured mile, which she covered at a speed of 29.75 knots. On the southward run the Queen herself took over at the wheel and kept the ship on course, this time covering the mile at 30 knots. As the vessel left Gourock for Southampton the following day, a collier hoisted the flag-signal 'What ship is that?' Sir James, answering, hoisted the *Queen Elizabeth*'s recognition flags giving GBSS, and, as she steamed in the Irish Sea a British submarine signalled 'What a beautiful target!' to which the *Queen Elizabeth* replied, 'I have been thinking that too, ever since I sighted you!'

On Wednesday, October 16 1946, the *Queen Elizabeth* was scheduled to sail on her first Atlantic voyage as a passenger ship. Publicity for that occasion was intense on both sides of the Atlantic and one writer described it thus:

BON VOYAGE

At last, young giant, infant of the fleet,
Your medals on, you sail down Civvy Street;
And may you serve the peaceful folk, you bring
As well, as nobly, as you served the King!
Here come your passengers, but who will check
The ghosts of soldiers crowding on your deck?

Sir A.P. Herbert

Epilogue

On April 2 1982, Argentinian forces invaded the Falkland Islands, part of the British Commonwealth. Immediately a British task force was sent to the South Atlantic to regain the territory. Many merchant vessels were requisitioned, among them several passenger ships including the *QE2*, the *Canberra*, and the *Norland*, which would serve as troop-ships, and the *Uganda* which was converted into a hospital ship. All the ships were refitted and many were equipped with a helicopter landing deck,

refuelling-at-sea points, and some of them with a desalination plant, to convert sea water into fresh, as well as highly advanced navigational equipment.

Many techniques from World War 2 were used again. The transports made their way out to the South Atlantic, with blackouts, zig-zags, escorts and radio silence enforced. On board the troops had to attend emergency drills, gun practices and, when reaching the 200-mile limit around the Falkland Islands, they had to sleep

Another time, another place, another ship. Queen Elizabeth 2, *like her predecessor, carries troops to yet another war-zone—the Falklands in 1982, troops at PT on her decks* (Soldier).

Queen Elizabeth 2 *on the alert off South Georgia Island, South Atlantic, May 1982.* RMS Canberra *is to the right of the picture, closer inshore* (Soldier).

fully clothed for passing this limit meant they came into range of enemy aircraft. These they all feared, the aircraft being jet-propelled and able to cover more than 1,000 miles within the hour, carrying a highly advanced and (theoretically) deadly accurate armament of missiles and bombs. Since the ships were not equipped with anti-aircraft devices, they depended for AA defence on the frigates and destroyers of their naval escort.

Their fears were realised when several of these escorts were hit and destroyed by Argentine missiles during numerous attacks. *Norland* and *Canberra* experienced many narrow escapes. Bombs fell close to the ships' bows and all the ships were sitting ducks for the Argentinian fighters when they were anchored in San Carlos Waters—re-named Bomb Alley. However, the *QE2* never entered the danger zone. She was anchored off South Georgia where her troops were trans-shipped to other vessels. She later returned to the UK carrying many of the wounded.

At the time of writing, the *QE2* and the *Canberra* are back in passenger service again. The conflict has ended and the British are in control

once again. However, after such an occurence, the question remains whether it still makes sense to think of using liners as troop transports, especially in the event of a major war.

Troop-ships which were available in World War 2, such as the *Queen Elizabeth*, the *Queen Mary, Nieuw Amsterdam* etc, relied on their speed. There were only a few vessels that could sail over 24 knots and even naval escorts were unable to keep up with the 28½ knots that the two *Queens* were capable of.

The oil crises of the 1970s together with the worldwide economic recession have spawned studies on more economical fuel consumption in ships' engines and now, cruising speeds in merchant vessels seldom surpass 19 knots. On the other hand, naval vessels have been developed to become faster and faster, using nuclear power with seemingly endless endurance, so that today even the *Queen Elizabeth*'s speed would not be able to compete against them.

The threat of submarine attack is now more dangerous than ever. Technologically advanced detection equipment, together with a vast range of torpedoes and missiles that can be launched while a submarine is submerged, will make any ship a sitting target for a submarine commander. Zigzagging will become useless in the future, for computers on board submarines will calculate what course will be followed.

Radar, which was a navigational novelty for the *Queen Elizabeth* could now become destructive for the transports. Its signals can be intercepted and are as likely to betray the ship's position as to discover an enemy.

But most of all, the Falklands war has proved that air power rules the waves as any ship nowadays is all too vulnerable to enemy aircraft, whether the ship is heavily armed or not. Missiles can be fired at a target from some twenty miles away and sophisticated devices make the missile able to find its own way to the target, with a precision of impact of 90 per cent.

Troop transportation on the World War 2 scale will never occur again, and newspaper bulletins stating that 500,000 troops could be carried across the Atlantic within a fortnight, will become part of legend.

The Falklands war proved that transporting troops overseas can only be handled if one of the parties is (a) superior in the number of naval vessels, supported by enough planes on aircraft carriers to defend ships against air attack and (b) is able to commandeer many merchant vessels, whilst the opposing party is unable to block the supply routes. Again, the Merchant Navy played a major role in warfare. Sir Percy Bates, in 1945, was right, perhaps, when he said he liked to believe that the two *Queens* had shortened the war by a whole year.

If a conflict arises between more countries or between nations which control the world's oceans, it will be very difficult to use ships for trooping purposes and perhaps a new design in Naval Auxiliary Vessels, similar to the *Norland* arrangement, and capable of carrying some 6,000 troops, plus military equipment, armed and armoured, will be more effective.

Almost forty years have elapsed since the end of World War 2, when conventional warfare created the conditions in which such transports as the *Queens* and many other ships operated, yet the Falklands crisis, coming in a so-called 'Push-Button Age', when the world thought transporting troops around the globe to be a thing of the past, showed that they were again all-important in a conflict of this nature. Maybe there is a lesson to be learned from this, that no power can afford to be caught out in relation to its maritime policy—fighting ships *and* merchantmen, it seems, still have a large part to play.

I wish I could convey the magnetic impression made on me by the sea. So vast, so boundless . . . grey-green distances . . . a tremendous mountainous heaving of a great breast.
Great creamy whitecaps . . . agate, marble-green-and-white swirling patterns as the great ship churned through the everlasting water.
The wave-peaks curl over white, and the wind blows the tops off in a straight streaming rush of hissing spray. The sea forever . . . not just a few hours, but days and nights of it . . . no land . . . only the great grey-white waters . . . limitless . . .
Awesome—inspiring—like the universe—beyond all comprehension

From a letter to his sister, dated December 21 1942, by James McDonald Gayfer.

Afterword by Walter Lord
(author of *A Night to Remember*)

Walter Lord was aboard the *Queen Elizabeth* during a voyage in 1944. He writes:

'I was one of 16,000 that the *Elizabeth* carried on that trip. I was going to Britain as a member of the OSS, our American intelligence agency at the time. Hoping to make us inconspicuous, the OSS had ordered us to dress in civilian clothes. That meant that there were 15,988 GI's in uniform on board and 12 men in grey flannel suits. You can imagine how inconspicuous we looked!

'Glenn Miller's band was also travelling with us, and the rumour spread that we must be members of the band—nobody could explain us any other way—and for a while we enjoyed quite a bit of undeserved attention and admiration. The band, incidentally, were all Air Force and, as a result, in uniform like everybody else.

'It was a fantastic trip. A lot of Cunard Line standard routine had lingered on despite the ship being converted to trooping duties. For instance, shortly before we arrived at Greenock I remember being told to fill out a form which included a question asking whether I planned to land at Cherbourg. At the time, Cherbourg was still in German hands, and I've often wondered what might have happened if I had checked "Yes".

'The following is an extract from a letter I wrote at the time:

"Our trip over was an unforgettable experience: There were 12 of us packed into a cabin designed for two. And there were other things to get used to as well, such as carrying your life-preserver around with you wherever you went, eating only two meals a day (even Bertha's consommé was better than no lunch at all), and never being allowed out on deck after dark. Time was largely spent reading, sleeping, and playing cards, all three of which were done standing up. The only public room was the officer's lounge, which was jammed with hundreds of officers and WACs at all hours of the day. These two main categories of personnel were theoretically separated by a rope, but there was a good deal of innocent liaison that went on beneath the barrier throughout the voyage. The crowds not only used all the chairs and tables but overflowed all over the floor. The whole scene was tinted with a heavy blue haze of tobacco smoke, and the sound effects consisted mainly of Coke bottles being opened and the jingle of coins changing hands in the inumerable games of Rummy and Blackjack. Contrary to all military legend and martial tradition, I did not see a single comic book the whole time I was on board." '

Walter Lord

Acknowledgements

First and foremost my sincere thanks and gratitude to: Oswald L. Brett, Levittown NY, USA, without whose time, devotion, recollections and original drawings much of this book would not have been possible; Frank O. Braynard, Sea Cliff, NY, USA, whose interest and confidence inspired me to seek publication; Mr P. de Kievit, former Dutch Mercantile Marine Officer, Rockanje, Holland, for his invaluable advice; my friends Hugh and Maureen Ghee, Blackpool, for their encouragement and help in the compilation of this book and Graham Truscott for his guidance at the publishers, Patrick Stephens Ltd.

Also, my thanks to the following for sharing their experiences and memories with me:

(Ex crew) **Australia:** James N. Delaney, Pymble, NSW; W.D. Heighway, Oatley, NSW; S.F. Hulme, Merriwa, NSW; Russel Nugent, Eastwood, NSW; Adrian Wheeler, Dover Heights, NSW; Alan Wickow, North Brighton, Victoria. **United States:** Walter Clarke, Nanuet, NY; Al Wakenshaw, Fort Lauderdale, Florida; Daniel Withey, Fairlawn, NJ.

(Ex troops) **Canada:** W.D. Adlam, Manotick, Ontario; E.A. Clark, Guelph, Ontario; J. Mc D. Gayfer, Lindsay, Ontario; R.O. Preston, Winnipeg, Manitoba. **United States:** R. Algaze, Colona del Mar, California; G.W. Anderson, Lake Michigan; E.N. Bailey, Durham, North Carolina; A. Borm, Freeland, Michigan; C.L. Brown, Spirit Lake, Idaho; T.L. Colacino, Newark, NY; G.T. Davis, Texarcana, Texas; A.S. Fontaine, Tallahassee, Florida; A. Grasso, Norwood, Massachusetts; G.M. Gurklies, Troy, Ohio; P.W. Holman Jr. Glasgow, Kentucky; D.W. Kendall, Muskegon, Michigan; H.R. McGuire, Williamsport, Pennsylvania; D. Patton, Crossville, Tennessee; F. Ryan Manasquan, NJ; H.J. Ritchie, Toms River, NJ; R. Scarpelli, Glendale, Arizona; W. Scholer, Tacoma, Washington; S. Sokel, Boca Raton, Florida; C.H. Sturdevant, Youngstown, Ohio; W.M. Tisch, Margate, Florida; R.J. Walsh, Augusta, Maine; R.D. Wolgamuth, Massachussetts;

For other invaluable material and advice: **Australia and New Zealand:** A.R. Bedwell, Auckland Harbour Board; W.Dunn, Brisbane, Queensland; Archives and Historical Studies (Navy), Canberra; National Library of Australia, Canberra; J.M. Mackenzie, Department of Defence, Canberra; Capt B.L. Noble, Fremantle Port Authority; P. Pinney, Brisbane, Queensland; A. White, Marine Board of Hobart. **Canada:** Public Archives, Ottawa; National Defence Headquarters, Ottawa; D.C. Holmes, Esquimalt Graving Dock, Victoria; Mrs J.C. Landry, Ottawa, Ontario; G.M. Mackay, Harbour Master Victoria and Esquimalt Public Harbours; Mrs V. Sinclair, Delta, British Columbia . **Egypt:** Ministry of Maritime Transport; Red Sea Ports Authority, Port Tewfik, Suez. **Germany:** Mr H. Maatz, Mönchengladbach; Militärgeschichtliches Forschungsamt, Freiburg im Breisgau; Deutches Rotes Kreuz, Suchdienst, München. **Holland:** Adrie Konings, Rockanje; Capt G. Koedijk, Oostvoorne; J.G. Kikkert, Oostvoone. **Ireland:** D.J. Kirwan, Limerick. **Sierra Leone:** Sierra Leone Ports Authority, Freetown. **South Africa:** Lt Cdr W.M. Bisset, SADF, Cape Town. **United Kingdom:** A.M. Ingham, Naval Ordnance Museum, R.N. Armament Depot, Gosport; Mrs V.J. Burgess, The British Library; Miss Pauline Fulcher, The Hull College of Higher Education; A. Hurst, Brighton; Mrs B. Marshall, Imperial War Museum, London; M. Cook, Archivist University of Liverpool, The Cunard Archive; Merseyside County Museum; Mr Paul Haley, *Soldier* magazine; Ministry of Defence, London; National Maritime Museum, Greenwich; I.M. Richards, Divisional Librarian, Central Library, Southampton; Mr Wm Miller, Scotland; *The Times*, London; Public Record Office, Kew,

Richmond; Peter Reekie, Cottingham; Lt Col J.K. Windeatt, Exeter; The Cunard Line, Southampton. **United States:** *DAV Magazine,* Mr Edward G. Gallian, New York; Library of Congress, Washington DC; Department of the Navy, Naval Historical Center, Washington DC; National Archives and Records Service, Washington DC; The Mariners Museum, Newport News;

Mr Jeff Blinn, Moran Towing and Transporting Co, New York; Mr S.R. Smith, Westboro, Massachusetts; Mr J. Splann, Naples, Florida; Mrs A.M. Werden, Mattoon, Illinois; Frank O. Braynard and Walter Lord.

For the wonderful patience, forbearance and selfless attitude shown to me at all times, my love and gratitude to my wife Gerda.

Bibliography

Behrens, C.B.A. *Merchant Shipping and the Demands of War;* London: Her Majesty's Stationery Office, 1955.

Bisset, Sir James. *'Commodore': War Peace and Big Ships;* London: Angus Robertson, 1961.

Brett, O.L. 'A Queen at War'; *Sea Breezes, Vol 20, 1955.*

Charles, R.W. *Troopships of World War II;* London: Olbourne, 1959.

Grattidge, Captain Harry. *Captain of the Queens;* London: Oldbourne, 1956.

Hutchinson, R. 'Cruising on the Queen E'; *Legion Magazine, Vol 56, no 9, 1982.*

King's Printer. *The Naval Service of Canada Vol III;* Ottawa: King's Printer, 1952.

Lacey, R. *The Queens of the North Atlantic;* London: Sidgwick and Jackson, 1978.

Maguire, Dr J.B. *The Sea my Surgery;* London:

Heinemann, 1957.

Potter, Neil and Frost, Jack. *The Elizabeth;* London: Harrap, 1965.

Potter, Neil and Frost, Jack. *The Queen Mary;* New York: The John Day Company, 1961.

Reader's Digest. 'Troopship'; *The Reader's Digest* March, 1944.

Shipbuilding and Shipping Record. Issues dated May 24 1945 and August 16 1945.

Time-Life. *De Passagiersschepen,* (originally by Melvin Maddocks); Time-Life International (Nederland) BV, 1979.

War and Navy Dept. *A short guide to Great Britain;* Washington: War and Navy Department, 1944.

Webster, M. 'The Queen Elizabeth at War'; *Sea Breezes,* Vol 47, 1973.

Index